THE WISDOM *of*
the LOTUS SUTRA

THE WISDOM OF THE

LOTUS SUTRA

A DISCUSSION

VOLUME II

EXAMINING CHAPTERS 3-10:

SIMILE AND PARABLE · BELIEF AND UNDERSTANDING
THE PARABLE OF THE MEDICINAL HERBS
BESTOWAL OF PROPHECY · THE PARABLE OF THE PHANTOM CITY
PROPHECY OF ENLIGHTENMENT FOR FIVE HUNDRED DISCIPLES
PROPHECIES CONFERRED ON LEARNERS AND ADEPTS
THE TEACHER OF THE LAW

Daisaku Ikeda
Katsuji Saito • Takanori Endo • Haruo Suda

World Tribune
—Press—

Published by
World Tribune Press
606 Wilshire Blvd.,
Santa Monica, CA 90401

© 2000 by the Soka Gakkai

ISBN 0-915678-70-5

Design by Gopa Design
Cover image © Photodisc

10 9 8 7 6 5 4 3 2

Library of Congress Cataloging-in-Publication Data

The Wisdom of the Lotus Sutra : a discussion : /
   Daisaku Ikeda... [et al].
      p. cm.
      Includes index.
      ISBN: 0-915678-70-5 (v. 2 : alk.paper)

      1. Tripitaka. Sutrapitaka.
   Saddharmapundarikasutra — Criticism.
   interpretation, etc. I. Ikeda, Daisaku.

   BQ2057.W57 2000   294.3'85—dc21
                       00-011670

Table of Contents

Editor's Note

This book is a series of discussions among SGI President Daisaku Ikeda, Soka Gakkai Study Department Chief Katsuji Saito and vice chiefs Takanori Endo and Haruo Suda. It was first serialized in English starting with the April 1995 issue of *Seikyo Times* (now *Living Buddhism*).

The following abbreviations appear in some citations:

✦ WND, page number(s) — refers to *The Writings of Nichiren Daishonin* (Soka Gakkai: Tokyo; 1999)

✦ GZ, page number(s) — refers to the *Gosho Zenshu*, the Japanese-language compilation of letters, treatises, essays and oral teachings of Nichiren Daishonin

✦ LS(chapter number), page number(s) — refers to *The Lotus Sutra*, translated by Burton Watson (Columbia University Press: New York; 1993)

PART ONE

"Simile and Parable" Chapter

1 Simile and Parable: Compassion and Wisdom Distilled to Their Fragrant Essence

Katsuji Saito: People often ask why the Lotus Sutra contains drawn-out passages describing inconceivably long periods of time—such as those which expound major world system dust particle *kalpas* and numberless major world system dust particle *kalpas*.

Takanori Endo: I often wonder the same thing. Numberless major world system dust particle *kalpas* is explained in the "Life Span" chapter. First, we are asked to imagine a person pulverizing to dust the astronomical number of five hundred, a thousand, ten thousand, a million *nayuta asamkhya*[1] thousand-millionfold worlds. Then the person proceeds to the east, dropping one speck each time he passes five hundred, a thousand, ten thousand, a million *nayuta asamkhya* worlds. Then Shakyamuni asks: "Good men, what is your opinion? Can the total number of all these worlds be imagined or calculated?" (LS16, 225).

Haruo Suda: On top of that, all those infinite numbers of worlds passed in this process are then also pulverized to dust, and each resulting particle of dust stands for one *kalpa*,[2] or aeon. This represents an enormously, unthinkably long period of time. It might indeed have been easier to express such numbers as one followed by x hundreds of zeros or ten to the xth power.

Daisaku Ikeda: Yes, and the Lotus Sutra would have ended up much shorter, then, wouldn't it!

But seriously, let's consider this. If the Buddha had said, "I became a Buddha ten-to-the-x-hundredth-power years ago," his listeners could only respond passively, "Yes, we see." But when this fact is presented to them as a narrative — "five hundred, a thousand, ten thousand, a million *nayuta asamkhya* worlds are pulverized to dust, and then one speck of the dust is dropped every five hundred, a thousand, ten thousand, a million *nayuta asamkhya* worlds" — the listeners are forced to form their own image of this incredibly long period, to think for themselves and actively assimilate this information.

Saito: I see. The many parables in the Lotus Sutra also attest to this power of the image to stimulate our minds.

Ikeda: Precisely. A certain educator once explained that when parables are used to teach, students follow the same path of thought that the teacher once followed. In other words, students don't simply listen passively to information but are encouraged to engage in the active mental process of thinking for themselves.[3]

Endo: In the treatment of psychological disorders, encouraging patients to think for themselves is also regarded as very important. There is, for example, the so-called sand-play therapy, in which patients are given a sandbox along with miniature houses, human figures and so on, and allowed to create their own little world. The process of creating their own narrative is thought to assist in activating the patients' inherent powers of self-healing.

Ikeda: We use the sand-play therapy in the educational counseling centers run by the Soka Gakkai's education division, don't we?

Saito: Yes. There are twenty-seven such educational counseling centers throughout Japan. In the twenty-seven years since the first one was opened, more than 200,000 people have availed themselves of this counseling service, and the program has been very well received.

Ikeda: Members of the education division provide a wonderful service, giving great encouragement to those with problems related to education. They are demonstrating the behavior of true bodhisattvas.

But to return to the Lotus Sutra, we all know that it is filled with memorable stories and parables. There are seven that are most outstanding and have come to be well known over the centuries. The first of the seven, the parable of the three carts and the burning house, appears in the "Simile and Parable" chapter. Today let us discuss the significance of parables centering on this chapter.

Suda: Perhaps we should begin with an overview of the entire chapter.

The Parable of the Three Carts and the Burning House

Endo: "Simile and Parable" begins with Shariputra's expression of his profound joy — the joy he feels after having heard and understood the teaching of the replacement of the three vehicles with the one vehicle, which was presented in the preceding "Expedient Means" chapter. Shariputra expressed his exaltation with his whole being. The sutra states: "Shariputra's mind danced with joy. Then he immediately stood up, pressed his palms together..." (LS3, 47). In other words, he leaps up with joy and presses his palms together in a gesture of reverence toward the Buddha. Nichiren Daishonin writes that this passage describes how one "dances with joy when one comes to the realization that the phenomena of the body and mind are the Mystic Law" (GZ, 722).

Saito: But the other disciples still don't understand. It is for their sake that Shariputra asks Shakyamuni to preach "a Law never known in the past" (LS3, 48). And Shakyamuni responds by preaching the parable of the three carts and the burning house.

Endo: As President Ikeda mentioned earlier, this is the first of the seven parables of the Lotus Sutra. The others are: the parable of the wealthy man and his poor son, which appears in "Belief and Understanding"; the parable of the three kinds of medicinal herbs and two kinds of trees, from "The Parable of the Medicinal Herbs"; the parable of the phantom city and the treasure land, from "The Parable of the Phantom City"; the parable of the gem in the robe, from "Prophecy of Enlightenment for Five Hundred Disciples"; the parable of the priceless gem in the topknot, from "Peaceful Practices"; and finally, the parable of the excellent physician and his sick children, from "Life Span."

Ikeda: Parables play a very important part not only in the "Simile and Parable" chapter but in the entire Lotus Sutra. As it says in "Expedient Means," "The marks of tranquil extinction borne by all phenomena / cannot be explained in words" (LS2, 44). The infinitely profound Law to which the Buddha has awakened is very difficult to put into words. Yet if that enlightenment remained locked in the Buddha's heart, the road to Buddhahood for all living beings would stay closed. The Buddha uses parables to preach the Law to open the way to enlightenment for all living beings.

Suda: I think now would be a good time to introduce the general outline of the parable of the three carts and the burning house.

In a certain town, there was an elderly man of considerable wealth. He owned a large mansion, but it was old and dilapidated. Suddenly the house caught fire, and soon the whole building was engulfed in flames. But the man's many children were still inside. Though the house was burning down around them and their lives were in great peril, the children were so engrossed in their games that they did not notice their predicament.

As the sutra says, "There is no safety in the threefold world; it is like a burning house" (LS3, 69). The burning house is a metaphor for this world of ours, enveloped as it is in the flames of suffering. The sutra describes the house with great vividness.

Endo: The house is infested with poisonous insects, snakes, rats, foxes, wolves, goblins, trolls, *yakshas* and evil spirits. Suddenly great walls of flame leap up, driving these creatures from their hiding places in wild and frenzied panic. One terrifying scene unfolds after another, just like a modern horror movie. Then the focus shifts to the children playing innocently, unaware of the dangers around them.

Ikeda: It's like watching the masterful camerawork of a gripping suspense movie. "Life is like a burning house" — this simile successfully stamps on our minds the powerful image of the dangers of a life lost in pleasure. The Lotus Sutra describes the sufferings of human existence in an extremely realistic fashion. That is one reason the Lotus Sutra has such a fine reputation as a work of literature.

The Chinese writer Lu Xun (1881–1936) used the image of the flames of the burning house to write his novel *Sihuo* (The Flame of Death).

Saito: This is a big difference from other Mahayana sutras, which tend to regard reality as an illusion. I think this is a defining characteristic of the Lotus Sutra, which stresses that all phenomena are one with the true aspect.

Ikeda: Yes, that's probably part of it. But the heart of the sutra is compassion, a determination to save all living beings, a profound empathy that feels the sufferings of other living beings as one's own.

Endo: The second half of the parable of the three carts and the burning house is just such a story of salvation. The wealthy man runs into the burning house and tells the children to leave at once. But the children, wrapped up in their games, aren't fazed by the burning house. They don't understand what it means to be burned alive, and so they keep running about the house, having fun.

The wealthy man devises a plan: He tells the children that outside he has placed goat-carts, deer-carts and ox-carts, things that they had wanted, and urges them to leave the house and choose whichever one they like. Hearing this, the children, each trying to be first, gleefully rush out of the conflagration to select their precious carts. And so it is that the children are all saved.

Suda: When the children demand the promised carts from their father, he gives them not goat-carts, deer-carts or ox-carts but presents each one with "a large carriage of uniform size and quality" (LS3, 57)—a magnificent jeweled carriage drawn by a white ox. The three kinds of carts he had originally promised—carts drawn by goat, deer or ox—stand for the three vehicles: The goat-cart is the teaching for voice-hearers (people of Learning); the deer-cart is the teaching for *pratyekabuddhas* (people of Realization); and the ox-cart is the teaching for bodhisattvas. But the great white ox cart that the father actually bestows on each of his children equally is the one Buddha vehicle—in other words, the teaching leading to Buddhahood.

Endo: Of course, the wealthy man in this parable is the Buddha, and the children playing in the house represent all living beings who do not recognize that they are in the midst of a world of suffering and will eventually be scorched by the flames of those sufferings.

The way the father gains the attention of his children with the three carts is a metaphor for the way the Buddha taught the three vehicles, shaping his teachings to match people's capacities in order to save them.

The fact that in the end the father gave each of his children a great white ox cart tells us that the Buddha's true teaching is not the three vehicles but the single Buddha vehicle.

Ikeda: The great white ox carts, representing the single Buddha vehicle, are described in great detail in the sutra. This description itself is a parable, an attempt to communicate the wonder of the state of Buddhahood.

Saito: The sutra calls them "large carriages adorned with seven kinds of gems" (LS3, 58). The wealthy man has many treasures in his storehouses, and he uses them to adorn the carriages with gold, silver, lapis lazuli, agate and other precious stones. These are great carts drawn by white oxen. The carriages had "railings running around them / and bells hanging from all sides. / Ropes of gold twisted and twined, / nets of pearls / stretched over the top" (LS3, 68).

Ikeda: This calls to mind the description of the jeweled stupa in "The Emergence of the Treasure Tower."

Suda: The white oxen that draw the carts are also beautiful. Their hides are pure and clean, and when they walk, they pull the carts straight and smoothly. When they run, they are as swift as the wind. The sutra says that the children, riding in these jeweled carts, enjoyed themselves in utter freedom.

Ikeda: This is a description of the state of Buddhahood. Offering the children the three carts to lure them from the burning house is the Buddha's act of relieving suffering. Presenting them with the great white ox carts is his act of conferring joy. He gave the children the state of unsurpassed ease and happiness — that is, the Buddha's wisdom.

"'I am the father of living beings and I should rescue them from their sufferings and give them the joy of the measureless and boundless Buddha wisdom so that they may find their enjoyment in that'" (LS2, 59).

The great white ox cart, which traverses freely over the most treacherous peaks, represents the state of Buddhahood, which knows no limitations. In "On the Great White Ox Cart," the Daishonin writes, "The great white ox cart is a vehicle that flies freely through the sky of the fundamental nature of the Law" (GZ, 1584).

The Daishonin remarks here that the description of the great white ox cart is abbreviated in Kumarajiva's Chinese translation of the Lotus Sutra. For his description of the magnificent vehicle, the Daishonin refers directly to a Sanskrit edition of the sutra.

Endo: As the Daishonin notes, the great white ox cart is five hundred *yojanas*[4] long, wide and high. This is even larger than the treasure tower that appears in the sutra's eleventh chapter. They are the same height, but the great white ox cart is twice as wide and as long as the treasure tower.

Suda: The Sanskrit text that the Daishonin refers to seems to be different from the surviving Sanskrit versions. But according to the Daishonin, it described the great white ox cart as having thirty-seven gleaming silver-thatched stairways leading up to it. Eighty-four thousand jeweled bells were hung on all four sides of the cart, and on the forty-two thousand railings, the Four Heavenly Kings[5] stood as guardians. Inside the cart, more than 69,380 Buddhas and bodhisattvas were sitting on lotus seats.

Ikeda: Such splendor defies the imagination. We certainly shouldn't imagine the great white ox cart as looking anything like the humble ox carts one used to see in the countryside long ago! Of course, you don't see them much anymore. I would be delighted if a gifted and inspired painter could depict this great white ox cart in all its glory.

Saito: The number 69,380 refers to the number of characters in the Chinese translation of the Lotus Sutra, doesn't it? In "The Opening of the Eyes," Nichiren Daishonin writes: "The Lotus Sutra is a single work consisting of eight volumes, twenty-eight chapters, and 69,384 characters. Each and every character is endowed with the character *myo*, each being a Buddha who has the thirty-two distinctive features and eighty characteristics"[6] (WND, 250).

Each character of the Lotus Sutra is a Buddha, and so 69,384 Buddhas are there inside the great white ox cart.

Ikeda: The great white ox cart is none other than the Lotus Sutra itself. Its substance is the wondrous life of the Buddha, the great life of Nam-myoho-renge-kyo. That is why the Daishonin writes, "The great white ox cart in the Lotus Sutra is the vehicle that I and other votaries of the Lotus Sutra are able to board" (GZ, 1584).

Endo: The splendid vision of the great white ox cart is also meant as a sharp contrast to the burning house.

Ikeda: Precisely. Living beings, submerged in foolishness and ignorance, not only fail to recognize that the house in which they dwell is actually burning up with them inside it but also fail to realize that their very lives contain the Buddha's life. Using parables, the Buddha seeks to awaken them to the brilliantly shining life inside them.

The Wide Influence
of the Lotus Sutra's Parables

Saito: There are many similes, parables and analogies in the Lotus Sutra, in addition to the seven we have already mentioned. The others most frequently referred to are: the great king's feast, in "The Bestowal of Prophecy"; the grinding of earth particles in the thousand-millionfold world into ink powder, in "Phantom City"; the digging of a well in a high plateau, in "The Teacher of the Law"; the grinding of five hundred, a thousand, ten thousand, a million *nayuta asamkhya* thousand-millionfold worlds to dust, in "Life Span"; the ten similes in "Former Affairs of the Bodhisattva Medicine King"; and the one-eyed turtle, in "Former Affairs of King Wonderful Adornment."

Of course, there are many more; far too many to cite here. Why is the Lotus Sutra so rich in parables and analogies? One apparent reason is the general fondness for parables and metaphor in Indian thought, but I think a more important reason is that the Lotus Sutra is a scripture that speaks to the people.

Suda: And, in fact, the marvelous parables of the sutra have fascinated and charmed many people, transcending boundaries and ages. Among the Chinese people, for example, faith in the Lotus Sutra stimulated the development of several genres of popular literature, recounting the benefits conferred on those who praised the Lotus Sutra and relating biographical accounts of sincere believers and practitioners of the sutra.[7] Clearly, it was the accessibility and illuminating nature of the parables of the Lotus Sutra that led to the emergence of such popular literature.

Endo: Though we don't possess enough evidence to draw a firm conclusion, some scholars suggest that the Lotus Sutra even influenced the New Testament of the Bible. For example, the story of the prodigal son in the Gospel according to Luke is very similar to the parable of the wealthy man and his poor son, which appears in the sutra's "Belief and Understanding" chapter.

Dr. Hajime Nakamura, the famous Japanese Buddhologist, refers to the possibility that Western religions espousing teachings of love may have developed under the influence of the Eastern ideal of compassion.[8]

Saito: In Japanese literature, too, the Lotus Sutra is the most frequently cited of all the many Buddhist scriptures. In the Nara period (710–94), shortly after Buddhism was introduced to Japan, the educated classes began to write poetry referring to Buddhist themes and ideas. But at this point, the Lotus Sutra was not yet widely adopted as a topic.

Among the common people, however, around this same time, the Lotus Sutra was becoming a subject of popular literature. In the *Nihon ryoiki*[9] (Miraculous Stories From the Japanese Buddhist Tradition), a collection of Buddhist tales recounting the karmic rewards and punishments of all sorts of people, the Lotus Sutra crops up with a frequency that far exceeds any other scripture.

Ikeda: In the Nara period, the Lotus Sutra was more favorably received among the common people than the elite. How appropriate for a scripture dedicated to helping people grapple with the realities of human existence!

Suda: From the time that Great Teacher Dengyo founded the Lotus Sutra-based Tendai school of Buddhism in Japan during the Heian period (794–1185), the Lotus Sutra came to be regarded as the king of the scriptures not only as a religious text but as a work of literature as well, even among the learned people of the capital. Lectures on the Lotus Sutra were regularly held in aristocratic society, and knowledge of the sutra was regarded as an indispensable part of one's general education.

Ikeda: In *The Pillow Book*, the Heian-period writer Sei Shonagon reveals the widespread currency of the Lotus Sutra among the nobility in a humorous anecdote.[10] The episode refers to Shakyamuni's statement in the "Expedient Means" chapter of the Lotus Sutra, when he responds to the departure of the five thousand arrogant believers from the assembly by saying, "It is well that these persons of overbearing arrogance have withdrawn" (LS2, 30). As Sei Shonagon prepared to leave a lecture on the Lotus Sutra, a certain nobleman named Fujiwara no Yoshichika remarked sarcastically, "Ah, you do well to depart!" To which she retorted, "Your Excellency, too, will surely be among the five thousand." It is clear from the ease with which Sei Shonagon and her friends bandied references to the Lotus Sutra that it had penetrated deeply into people's consciousness at this time.

Suda: The Lotus Sutra is also the most frequently cited Buddhist scripture in Murasaki Shikibu's *The Tale of Genji,* regarded by many as the world's first novel. Among the various Buddhist ceremonies that the characters of the novel hold, the custom of the Eight Lectures on the Lotus Sutra[11] is frequently mentioned.

The novel's leading character, Hikaru Genji, is said at the age of twenty-three to have read the three main Tendai scriptures[12] and their many commentaries—sixty volumes in all—and so was deeply versed in the Lotus Sutra.

Saito: Some scholars say that a well-known scene in "The Broom Tree" chapter follows the structure of the three cycles of preaching[13] of the Lotus Sutra.

Endo: From the mid-Heian period on, the emperor and the aristocracy often composed poems based on various Lotus Sutra chapters. This custom of writing a poem based on a single chapter seems to have been popular in China and was transmitted from there to Japan. According to scholars of Japanese literature, the "Expedient Means" and "Life Span" chapters were the most frequent choices for such poems, followed by the "Devadatta" chapter and those chapters in which the seven parables are expounded:

"Simile and Parable," "Belief and Understanding," "The Parable of the Medicinal Herbs," and "Prophecy of Enlightenment for Five Hundred Disciples."

For example, the following poem is based on the parable of the gem in the robe, from the "Five Hundred Disciples" chapter:

> *I only learned*
> *By a chance meeting*
> *With an old friend*
> *Of the jewel sewn in my robe*
> *While I was drunk.*[14]

Another poem alludes to the parable of the three carts and the burning house:

> *The world is a dismal place*
> *And yet how*
> *Am I to escape*
> *This house of burning desires*
> *Without the ox cart?*[15]

Ikeda: The Lotus Sutra was so well known among the populace at this time that many of its famous phrases were incorporated in puns within poetry.

THE DISTINCTIVE FEATURES OF THE PARABLES

Suda: Where, I wonder, does this tremendous power of the Lotus Sutra's parables to captivate people's hearts and imaginations come from? In particular, the sutra devotes eight of its twenty-eight chapters to clarifying the true function of the three vehicles and replacing them with the one Buddha vehicle, thereby emphasizing that all living beings possess the potential for Buddhahood. Five of the Lotus Sutra's seven parables are found in these eight chapters. This teaching is set forth with such persist-ence that some might find it a little tiresome. But what we see here, I think, is the extraordinary depth of Shakyamuni's com-passion.

Ikeda: Exactly. That is precisely the source of the richness of the parables of the Lotus Sutra.

The Great Teacher T'ien-t'ai of China comments: "The Bud-dha's great compassion is never exhausted, his skillful wisdom operates without limit. That is why the Buddha preaches para-bles. Moving the trees, he shows us the wind; raising his fan, he reveals the moon. This is how he awakens us to the truth."[16]

Nichiren Daishonin quotes this passage and adds his own com-ment: "[The Buddha's] 'great compassion' is like the mercy and compassion a mother feels for her child" (GZ, 721). It is deep com-passion that gives birth to these skillful parables. He further cites the words of T'ien-t'ai's disciple Chang-an: "One who rids the offender of evil is acting as his parent" (GZ, 721).

The Daishonin is describing the strict love of a parent who will fight to rid his or her child of evil, even if it means earning the child's dislike.

> "[N]ow this threefold world
> is all my domain,
> and the living beings in it
> are all my children.
> Now this place
> is beset by many pains and trials.
> I am the only person
> who can rescue and protect others,…" (LS3, 69–70)

Saito: can see the parental concern of the Buddha here and there throughout the "Simile and Parable." For example, Shakyamuni states: "These living beings are all my sons. I will give the Great Vehicle to all of them equally" (LS3, 61); and "Now this threefold world / is all my domain, / and the living beings in it / are all my children" (LS3, 69).

Suda: The last passage is a very important one, for it makes the relation between the Buddha and living beings perfectly clear.

Ikeda: All seven of the central Lotus Sutra parables reveal the compassion of the Buddha for living beings. In three of them—the parables of the three carts and the burning house, the wealthy man and his poor son, and the excellent physician and his sick children —the Buddha is depicted as a father who saves his children.

In the parable of the three kinds of medicinal herbs, he is likened to a great cloud of compassion that delivers rain equally to all types of plants; in the parable of the phantom city and the treasure land, he is depicted as a caravan leader; in the parable of the gem in the robe, he is depicted as a man who protects his friend; and in the parable of the priceless gem in the topknot, he is depicted as a king who praises his minister.

The parables are not preached 'in accordance to the mind of living beings,' matching their capacities. They are preached 'in accordance with the Buddha's own mind,' to reveal that mind and to draw living beings toward it. The Daishonin writes: "But the Lotus Sutra is an example of preaching in accordance with the Buddha's own mind, because in it the Buddha had all living beings comply with his own mind"(WND, 969).

The parables of the Lotus Sutra are taught to make the minds of living beings one with the Buddha's mind.

Saito: The parables of the Lotus Sutra have the power to raise living beings to the state of Buddhahood.

Ikeda: Yes, they do. Earlier I noted that parables have the power to make one think in a very active and participatory way. Tsunesaburo Makiguchi designed his educational system to achieve that same effect. I am referring to what he called a "home environment course" and "practical education." His idea was to lead students to experience what they could in their own home environment and then move on to learn things they couldn't directly experience, always using their own experience as a reference point. With the students' actual experiences serving as parables, as it were, Mr. Makiguchi's method encourages students to expand their field of thought on their own. That is why he placed such importance on free activities for students.

Using easily understandable parables and similes to teach is the same as guiding students to think on their own. And it is precisely this that brings about a dramatic change in those being taught.

Related to this, a certain person once described the seven parables of the Lotus Sutra as medicine to cure the illnesses of life. I am speaking of the Indian Buddhist philosopher Vasubandhu, active around the fourth or fifth century.

Vasubandhu stated, for instance, that the parable of the three carts and the burning house is a cure for the arrogant mind that mistakenly seeks every kind of virtue. "Mistakenly" here refers to the folly of seeking true happiness in the burning house of this threefold world.

The parable of the phantom city and the treasure land, said Vasubandhu, is a cure for the arrogant mind convinced of the reality of things that do not actually exist or have substance. It specifically teaches the voice-hearers that the limited enlightenment of the two vehicles, which they believe to be everything, is in fact no more than a phantom city—in other words, that it doesn't exist.

The parable of the gem in the robe, meanwhile, cures the arrogant mind convinced that that which is true or real isn't real. It teaches that the jewel (the Buddha nature) that living beings do not believe exists is there all along, sewn into the lining of their robes (inherent in their very lives).

Thus, Vasubandhu described the seven parables as beneficial medicine for curing the illnesses of life. And Shakyamuni, by that token, is a great doctor who cures and revives living beings. He is a great doctor and a strict father. In all of his incarnations, what shines through is Shakyamuni's ardent compassion, which seeks to make all living beings happy.

Saito: The parable of the excellent physician and his sick children in the "Life Span" chapter shows the Buddha as both the great doctor and the strict father.

Ikeda: The Buddha of the "Life Span" chapter is the Buddha who works ceaselessly for the salvation of all beings—from the beginningless past and on into the endless future. The life of this Buddha is eternal, and yet he appears in the world to save living beings and then enters extinction again for the same purpose. His appearance and extinction are all for the sake of living beings. This Buddha is the perfect expression of a life of compassion.

Endo: In the first of the seven parables, the three carts and the burning house, the Buddha is depicted as a father. The passage mentioned earlier, "Now this threefold world / is all my domain, / and the living beings in it / are all my children" (LS3, 69), illustrates the compassionate determination of the Buddha, who is the father, to save all living beings, who are his children. This Buddha who acts as a father to all living beings is then revealed in the "Life Span" chapter as the Buddha of time without beginning, who represents the eternal function and activity of compassion.

Ikeda: "The One Hundred and Six Comparisons" refers to this passage as a hidden reference to the "Life Span" chapter (GZ, 856).

PARABLES ARE IDENTICAL TO THE ENTITY OF THE LAW

Suda: The similes and parables that appear in the Lotus Sutra have another very important feature. Not only does Shakyamuni employ them in his attempts to convey the profound depths of the teachings of the Lotus Sutra to his disciples, but his disciples use them, too, to demonstrate that they have understood his teachings.

When we think of using parables to explain something, we usually consider it as a method employed by a teacher when instructing his students. But in the Lotus Sutra, parables are by no means a one-way street; the Buddha's disciples also use parables when they speak.

Saito: For example, the four great voice-hearers,[17] who immediately grasped the meaning of the parable of the three carts and the burning house, reveal their understanding in "Belief and Understanding" by relating the parable of the wealthy man and his poor son. While in "Prophecy of Enlightenment for Five Hundred Disciples," the voice-hearers, who have grasped the teaching of causes and conditions set forth in "The Parable of the Phantom City," show their understanding by sharing the parable of the gem in the robe.

Ikeda: Simply hearing the Buddha's skillful parables and similes and declaring, "Yes, I understand!" do not constitute a full understanding. Truly profound understanding results in a transformation of one's entire being. By its very nature, understanding entails a transformation. As one rises to a higher state of being, wisdom is born. That is why the disciples who heard and truly understood the Buddha's teachings could then speak in parables themselves.

We must also remember that Shakyamuni used parables to reach all living beings. His purpose was to open the path of Buddhahood to all without exception. Once his disciples understood the meaning behind the parables, the reason why the Buddha used them, it seems quite natural that they would respond with parables of their own. The joy of understanding filled them with an irrepressible desire to share this truth with others.

Endo: In a different context entirely, this "joy of understanding" reminds me of the story of the ancient Greek mathematician and inventor Archimedes' discovery of the physical law of buoyancy known as Archimedes' Principle.

The king wanted to confirm whether a certain crown was in fact made of pure gold, and he asked Archimedes to find out for him—without, of course, damaging the crown. Archimedes went to the public bath to puzzle over this problem when he noticed, as he lowered himself into the tub, that the water overflowed. At that instant, a way of measuring the gold struck him like a bolt of lightning. He leapt out of the bath and cried "Eureka! Eureka!" (I've found it!). This episode is quite famous, and the term *eureka* has been an expression for the joy of discovery throughout the West for centuries.

Ikeda: No doubt it is because Archimedes' jubilation continues to pulse in this expression that it has survived over the centuries down to the present day. Likewise, the uncontainable joy of the Buddha's disciples permeates the parables they offer.

Interestingly, Shakyamuni tells Shariputra that he is preaching the Lotus Sutra to make him recall the Buddha way, which the latter had aspired to and practiced in the past. The Buddha states: "Now, because I want you to recall to mind the way that you originally vowed to follow,... I am preaching this Great Vehicle sutra called the Lotus of the Wonderful Law" (LS3, 51).

Understanding and conveying the truth to others are acts of remembering. Recollection is possible because the truth is already within one's life. That is why the Lotus Sutra places such importance on both parables and the influence of causes and conditions. The "Life Span" chapter teaches the ultimate causes and conditions dating back to the beginningless past.

Saito: The Japanese poet Makoto Ooka writes:

> The words we use in everyday speech can suddenly assume, depending upon the ways in which they are

combined or the moments in which they are uttered, a tremendous power.... The language we use is like the tip of an iceberg. What is the part of the iceberg that rests below the ocean surface? It is the intent, the mind of the person who speaks the language, and the mind of the listener, to which the word communicates, also below the ocean's surface of language.[18]

Ikeda: In a sense, when we use a parable, we are changing the ways in which we usually combine words, selecting expressions that perfectly communicate our message. When we do this, ordinary, familiar words and phrases take on a new meaning that transcends their typical uses. They acquire a power to link the minds and character of people that are submerged and exist on a level deeper than language.

This communication is the real meaning of understanding and conveying ideas. And this is why parables have such power.

Endo: To share one of my own experiences, I remember once being really down in the dumps, and one of my seniors said to me simply, "It's been really tough, hasn't it?" I felt that very ordinary phrase as a great encouragement, and I was deeply moved. It's amazing how our sincere concern for another can be so moving, can have such a great effect.

Ikeda: Yes. They are words, but they are more than words. The power of words derives from the human heart. The mind, the heart, is what lies at the bottom of words and what gives them life. Nichiren Daishonin observes, "Words manifest through sound to convey the sentiments in our hearts" (GZ, 563). The same words can have very different degrees of power, too, depending upon the depth of the hearts of those who speak them.

In one of his commentaries, the Great Teacher Dengyo writes, "These seven parables [of the Lotus Sutra] are none other than the entity of the Law, and the entity of the Law is none other than these metaphors and parables" (WND, 426). This means that the Lotus Sutra parables are the very heart and mind of the Buddha. In "The Entity of the Mystic Law," the Daishonin elucidates that Nam-myoho-renge-kyo is the ultimate expression of this principle that the parables of the Lotus Sutra are identical to the entity of the Law.

Suda: In the past, the Lotus Sutra has been criticized for lacking doctrinal teachings and constituting nothing more than a collection of parables and lavish praise for the Buddha.

Ikeda: Japanese scholars such as Tominaga Nakamoto and Hirata Atsutane are well known for voicing such criticisms.

Suda: After studying the Lotus Sutra, the Edo-period philosopher Tominaga concluded that it contained little more than praise for the Buddha and presented no teachings worth mentioning. He also criticized the parables of the sutra for merely emphasizing the superiority of the sutra itself.

Hirata, a scholar of Japanese classics, declared the Lotus Sutra to be inferior to all other Mahayana scriptures. Compared to the other Mahayana sutras, he said, it was decidedly unsatisfying, having no real substance; it was filled with warnings about the destruction of Buddhism and had many fantastic tales but never stated its purpose.

According to Hirata, the only thing one could say for the twenty-eight chapters was that they were long and, though they were filled with praise for the remedy they promised, they never actually delivered the medicine they touted.

Ikeda: Nichiren Daishonin wrote something that seems at first glance to be of similar intent: "Bear in mind that the twenty-eight chapters of the Lotus Sutra contain only a few passages elucidating the truth, but a great many words of praise" (WND, 673). But the Daishonin's conclusion is the opposite of Hirata's. He asserts,

"The more one praises the blessings of the Lotus Sutra, the more one's own blessings will increase" (WND, 673).

The Daishonin is suggesting that we adopt the position of the Buddha. Since the Buddha praises the Lotus Sutra, we are bound to reap great benefit if we do the same. It means embracing the Buddha's spirit as our own. Unless we have this attitude—that is, unless we have faith—we will never understand the Lotus Sutra, which expounds the Buddha's heart and intent. Indeed, when we read the Lotus Sutra with the heart of faith, it is immediately clear how shallow such criticisms of it are.

For in those "few passages elucidating the truth," of which the Daishonin speaks, the seed of Buddhahood for all living beings is indisputably present.

Suda: Contemporary scholars also point out that the objections of Tominaga and others to the Lotus Sutra are ill-founded. For example, Dr. Nakamura, whom we cited earlier, writes:

> There is no systematic presentation of an abstract phi-
> losophy in the first half of the Lotus Sutra. It restricts
> itself to a repeated, richly expressed assertion, employ-
> ing a variety of parables, of the doctrine that all of the
> Buddha's teachings are solely the one Buddha vehicle.
> As a result, anyone who seeks a particular philosophical
> or doctrinal system in this part of the sutra will be dis-
> appointed. But it is this very absence of a specifically
> stated philosophy that indicates the Lotus Sutra's impor-
> tant philosophical position.[19]

Saito: Earlier, through the parables, we discussed the power of language to encourage and enlighten. But in our society today, unfor-
tunately, language is frequently put to other purposes: to deceive,
to exploit, and to render insensible people's awareness of basic
human rights.

Suda: Mr. Toda declared, "Speech or writing bereft of conviction is as insubstantial as smoke." When we see smoke, we can evade it. But in Japan today, public discourse is so engulfed in the smoke of lies that there is nowhere to escape."

No one even tries any more.

Ikeda: We live, if not in a burning house, in a smoking house!

Suda: Dr. Toshio Kamba, a noted sociologist and professor at Soka University, once noted: "The ruling elites of government and business are trying to bring the media under their control in order to steer public opinion in a direction favorable to their own agendas...."[20] And he warned:

> It is crucial that such fascist political tendencies are nipped in the bud, before they can take firm hold. Japan's prewar experience taught us that a repressive government begins by instituting relatively mild measures of control. But it quickly picks up the tempo and organizes its forces. Once that has happened, a great deal of effort is required to oppose the rise of fascism. And that is why we must strike hard against the conservative reactionary forces now, when they are just beginning to exercise their power.[21]

Ikeda: That's true. We must be alert to the forces running beneath the smallest changes in society. And we must nip evil in the bud and encourage the growth of good. Every phenomenon has implications that must be understood, and every phenomenon can be transformed into a productive development, into something of ultimate value.

At the closing lines of his tragedy *Faust,* Goethe writes that all that is changeable is but an eternal parable.[22]

Saito: It is easy enough for us, too, if we're not careful, to fall victim to the illusion that the most profound essence of Buddhism is to be found in some theory or doctrine separated from our daily lives, but the parables of the Lotus Sutra teach us that this real world before us is true Buddhism.

Ikeda: The proof of faith that we manifest in our lives represents parables or illustrations of the virtues to be obtained from embracing the Mystic Law. Such proof is an eloquent testimony to the truth of the Mystic Law.

The great examples of Shijo Kingo, the two Ikegami brothers and other disciples of Nichiren Daishonin who faced and overcame great difficulties in their pursuit of faith are a tremendous encouragement to us who face similar problems. The Daishonin encouraged the Ikegami brothers when the two united in the face of persecution, writing, "Could there ever be a more wonderful story than your own?" (WND, 499). And just as the Daishonin asserted, the story of the brothers is now told around the world.

The same applies to us. Our individual experiences of triumph over our problems give courage and hope to many others. Our personal victories, in other words, become parables expressing the power of the Mystic Law. And those who hear our experiences can share them with still others.

Mr. Makiguchi started the Soka Gakkai's discussion meeting movement, which centers on members sharing their experiences in faith with others. He taught the Mystic Law not in the form of difficult abstract theories but through easily intelligible personal experiences.

Each individual experience is a parable of the all-pervading Mystic Law. And the discussion meeting, based on sharing such personal experiences, is a contemporary representation of the "Simile and Parable" chapter, a modern version of the seven parables of the Lotus Sutra, an infinite treasury of parables.

Parables are wisdom and compassion distilled to their most fragrant essence. The Soka Gakkai initiated a revolution in the way Buddhism is spread by adopting the same method as the Lotus

Sutra. The spirit of the Lotus Sutra's parables lives on in the sixty-five–year history of the Soka Gakkai. And we will continue to write the brilliant story of the widespread propagation of the Lotus Sutra (Nam-myoho-renge-kyo) day after day, a story that will be passed down through eternal future generations.

NOTES

1. *Nayuta* and *asamkhya* (both Sanskrit terms) are ancient Indian numerical units, whose explanations differ according to the source. One source defines them respectively as 10^{11} and 10^{59}.

2. *Kalpa*: (Skt) An extremely long period of time. Sources differ somewhat in their definitions. According to one, a small *kalpa* is approximately 16 million years.

3. From the Japanese translation of Otto Friedrich Bollnow's *Sprache und Erziehung:* O.F. Bollnow, *Gengo to Kyoiku* (Language and Education), trans. Takashi Morita (Tokyo: Kawashima Shoten, 1969), p. 165.

4. *Yojana*(s): (Skt) A measurement unit of ancient India, equal to the distance the royal army was thought to be able to march in a day. Approximations vary as widely as 9.6, 16 and 24 kilometers.

5. Four Heavenly Kings: Lords of the four quarters who serve Indra (Jpn Taishaku) as his generals and protect the four continents.

6. Thirty-two distinctive features and eighty characteristics: The remarkable physical characteristics and extraordinary features possessed by Buddhas and bodhisattvas.

7. Such Chinese works as *The Lotus Sutra and its Traditions* and *Wide Praise for the Lotus Sutra.*

8. Hajime Nakamura, "Indo to Girishia to no Shiso Koryu" (Intellectual Exchange Between India and Greece), *Nakamura Hajime Senshu* (Selected Works of Hajime Nakamura) (Tokyo: Shunjusha, 1968), vol. 16, p. 191.

9. *Miraculous Stories from the Japanese Buddhist Tradition:* The Nihon ryoiki

of the Monk Kyokai, trans. and ed. Kyoko Motomochi Nakamura (Cambridge: Harvard University Press, 1973).

10. *The Pillow Book of Sei Shonagon,* trans. Ivan Morris (London: Oxford University Press, 1967), p. 39.

11. Eight Lectures on the Lotus Sutra: Refers to the custom of holding lectures on the eight volumes of the Lotus Sutra in eight sessions by eight diVerent people.

12. The three main Tendai (T'ien-t'ai) scriptures: *Profound Meaning of the Lotus Sutra, Words and Phrases of the Lotus Sutra* and *Great Concentration and Insight.*

13. Three cycles of preaching: The cycles of preaching, understanding and prediction of enlightenment that Shakyamuni employed in the Lotus Sutra. The cycles are repeated in accord with the different capacities of each of the three groups of voice-hearer disciples.

14. The poem is by Senshi Naishinno, which is included in the *Hosshin Waka Shu,* a collection of fifty-five poems based on the Lotus Sutra. The charm of the poem in the original derives largely from untranslatable puns.

15. Author anonymous. Included in the *Shui Waka Shu* (Collection of Gleanings), an imperial anthology of *waka* poems completed between 996–1007.

16. *Words and Phrases of the Lotus Sutra,* vol. 5.

17. The four great voice-hearers: Maudgalyayana, Mahakashyapa, Katyayana and Subhuti.

18. Makoto Ooka, *Shi, Kotoba, Ningen* (Poetry, Words and People) (Tokyo: Kodansha Gakujutsu Bunko, 1985), p. 28.

19. Hajime Nakamura, "Indo Shiso no Shomondai" (Observations on Indian Thought), *Nakamura Hajime Senshu* (Selected Works of Hajime Nakamura) (Tokyo: Shunjusha, 1968), vol. 10, pp. 216–17.

20. Toshio Kamba, *Rekishi wa kurikaesu ka?* (Does History Repeat Itself?) (Tokyo: Keiso Shobo, 1979), p. 86.

21. Ibid., pp. 207–08.

22. cf. German and Japanese translations of Johann Wolfgang von Goethe's *Faust.*

PART TWO

"Belief and Understanding" Chapter

2 Belief and Understanding: The Dynamic Relationship of Faith and Wisdom

Saito: The subtheme of our discussion on the Lotus Sutra is "Religion in the Twenty-first Century." President Ikeda, you participated in a discussion on this theme. It was in your meeting with Professor Lawrence E. Sullivan of Harvard University in March 1993. I was particularly impressed by your ideas concerning religion in the twenty-first century. You emphasized that there should be a kind of open competition among religions to determine which one best serves people's needs. And you noted that Buddhism offers three proofs upon which that peaceful competition may be based: documentary proof, theoretical proof and actual proof.

You also stated that a religion has a natural life span, and that people ought not to cling to dead religions, a conclusion that was particularly startling to me. The people, you said, are the ones who decide what the truth is. I remember thinking, "This is the correct Buddhist view of the role of the people and the nature of religion."

Endo: I'm afraid I would have simply declared that, when it comes right down to it, the Buddhism of Nichiren Daishonin is the only religion.

Saito: It's true that we may tend to leap to that conclusion. What really moved me was the point that the people themselves should be the ones to decide the particulars of religion in the twenty-first century. And at the same time, no religion can be called a true religion of the people unless people choose it on their own initiative, thinking for themselves and exercising wisdom.

Suda: Yes, that's true. Let's assume for the sake of argument that there is a highly capable political leader who decides that a particular religion is correct. And because he feels it is "the truth," for the people's sake, he makes his choice the state religion and decrees that all citizens must take faith. This might be extreme, but such a religion is not likely to take root among the people. Even if a religion is correct, if it is forced on people and given a privileged place in society by the powers that be, this will spell its death. Such a state of affairs will in turn spell an end to people's spiritual freedom.

Ikeda: That's right. The idea of forcing people to accept a particular religion is entirely foreign to Buddhism. King Ashoka (R.C. 268–32 B.C.E.) of India, for example, was a fervent Buddhist, but he adopted a policy of tolerance toward all faiths.

When Nichiren Daishonin returned from exile in Sado, he refused to accept the government's offer to build a temple for him. He had no wish whatsoever to be supported by the government.

Endo: The Daishonin believed that the balance of power ought to lie with the people, not the authorities. And this is more true now than it was then.

Saito: I wonder how Japan today measures up to that ideal. Are the people becoming wise? Are they thinking for themselves? No. There are those who take advantage of that ignorance to fan their mistrust and anxiety. In the end the people are blind to the government's attempts to regulate and control religion. In the calls for stricter government control of "bad" religions, we see a lack of awareness of the government's potential to abuse power and, hence, the immaturity of Japan's democracy.

Suda: The journalist Karel Van Wolferen warns that the true intention of Japan's leaders is to keep the people ignorant. Unless the Japanese people wake up, they will play right into the hands of the authorities who want nothing more than to keep them ignorant so that these authorities can continue doing as they please.

Ikeda: The SGI is a gathering of ordinary people. We struggle to ensure that the people are not despised and exploited by the powerful. To help all people become strong and wise, we are developing a network of peace and culture and putting great effort into education. By nature, the people are strong, wise, cheerful and warm. Religious faith has the power to draw out those qualities. The purpose of faith is not to turn people into sheep; it is to make them wise. Wisdom isn't knowledge that causes suffering for others; it is enlightened insight for improving one's own life as well as the lives of others.

I think that today's societal distortions derive from a confusion of wisdom, which is holistic, and knowledge, which is fragmentary, as well as an inability to distinguish genuine from blind belief. Nichiren Daishonin says, "The character *myo* means to open" (WND, 145). Life naturally tends toward the opening of full potential, toward limitless advancement. The function of the Mystic Law, of a true religion, is to enable people to manifest that tendency to the highest degree. And faith is the key that enables us to open the full potential of our lives, our inherent wisdom. The Daishonin says, "'To open' is another name for faith" (GZ, 716).

Kumarajiva[1] renders the inborn spirit of continually seeking self-improvement as "belief and understanding," the title of the Lotus Sutra's fourth chapter. Simply put, "belief and understanding" means to fully accept and understand. People must be able to accept and understand the teachings. That is the kind of faith that the Lotus Sutra teaches; it is by no means blind. In this chapter, let's discuss what faith is and what it means to believe in light of the "Belief and Understanding" chapter.

THE PARABLE OF THE WEALTHY MAN AND HIS POOR SON AND THE AWAKENING OF THE FOUR GREAT MEN OF LEARNING

> We today have heard
> the Buddha's voice teaching
> and we dance for joy,
> having gained what we never had before.
> The Buddha declares that the voice-hearers
> will be able to attain Buddhahood.
> This cluster of unsurpassed jewels
> has come to us unsought....
> Now we have become
> voice-hearers in truth,
> for we will take the voice of the Buddha way
> and cause it to be heard by all. (LS4, 87–94)

Saito: "Belief and Understanding" begins with men of Learning (voice-hearers) rejoicing at Shakyamuni's teaching that the people of the two vehicles (Learning and Realization) will attain Buddhahood. In "Simile and Parable," the third chapter, Shakyamuni assures Shariputra that in a future age called Great Treasure Adornment, he will be born in the land Free From Stain as a Buddha named Flower Glow Thus Come One (cf. LS3, 51–52). In the Mahayana sutras that Shakyamuni had previously expounded, the voice-hearers and *pratyekabuddhas* were disdained and the possibility of their enlightenment denied. But here in the Lotus Sutra, Shakyamuni for the first time explains that they, too, can attain Buddhahood.

Endo: Hearing that, the four great men of Learning express their joy. They are Subhuti, foremost in the understanding of the doctrine of nonsubstantiality; Mahakatyayana, foremost in debate; Mahakashyapa, foremost in the practice to eliminate desires; and Mahamaudgalyayana, foremost in supernatural powers. When they "heard the World-Honored One prophesy that Shariputra would attain anuttara-samyak-sambodhi [Skt; supreme enlightenment], their minds were moved as seldom before and [they] danced for joy" (LS4, 80). The "Belief and Understanding" chapter records their joy at hearing "a Law that they had never known before" (LS4, 80).

Suda: These four were central figures in the Buddhist community —senior leaders, as it were. But they were "old and decrepit" and, as they admit, "believed that we had already attained nirvana and that we were incapable of doing more, and so we never sought to attain anuttara-samyak-sambodhi" (LS4, 81).

Ikeda: They had positions to maintain. They had seniority and experience. And so they had become complacent. They had practiced for many years and grown old. They had attained a certain degree of enlightenment and were satisfied with it. While acknowledging that the enlightenment of their mentor, Shakyamuni, was indeed wondrous, they had reconciled themselves to the notion that they could never achieve anything comparable. Therefore, they were happy to remain as they were. But then the prediction of Shariputra's enlightenment broke through the complacency of these leaders. In the mirror of the Lotus Sutra, we find an image of continuous and impassioned lifelong pursuit of the Way.

Saito: Some sources suggest that Shariputra was actually older than Shakyamuni. That would mean that when Shakyamuni preached the Lotus Sutra, Shariputra must have been around eighty years old. A Sanskrit version of the Lotus Sutra says that the four great men of Learning "sat near the World-Honored One for so many years that their bodies ached, their joints were brittle.... and they were old and weak."[2]

Suda: Then their teacher, Shakyamuni, turns to them and tells them they still have much to achieve and urges them to keep trying.

Ikeda: He teaches them the practice of eternal self-improvement and calls on them to determine never to retreat. "Not advancing is retreating" (GZ, 1165). Buddhist practice means continually working to improve oneself and one's surroundings, advancing ever forward. It means eternal growth and, therefore, eternal youth. Life is eternal, continuing throughout past, present and future.

Endo: The disciples of the two vehicles also confess that they have cast a cold eye on the efforts of the bodhisattvas to transform society and guide the people based on the Buddha's teaching.

Ikeda: The practitioners of the two vehicles had succumbed to a kind of inner death. Not only did they not desire to become Buddhas themselves, but they looked askance on those striving to attain Buddhahood. They divorced themselves from such aspirants and ridiculed them. That's why some Mahayana sutras describe them as "having scorched the seeds for attaining Buddhahood." But, at the most basic level, the Buddha does not abandon the practitioners of the two vehicles. He admonishes and encourages them, saying: "See here, this won't do. This is not who you really are. You can attain a higher and more blissful state of being."

Saito: The Sanskrit version of the Lotus Sutra says, "The practitioners of the two vehicles, though they did not themselves seek the supreme enlightenment of the Buddha, taught and admonished the bodhisattvas to attain the Buddha's supreme enlightenment."[3]

Ikeda: Urging others to accomplish what we do not attempt to achieve ourselves is outrageous. It's incredibly arrogant. The tendency to make others do something while personally neglecting to make the same effort is a pitfall of "organizationism." With such cowards for leaders, any organization will become calcified. Most important, such people stop growing themselves. And when life stagnates, it sickens.

In the Lotus Sutra, the practitioners of the two vehicles accept Shakyamuni's rebuke and his encouragement heart and soul. Only then are they "reborn" as "voice-hearers in truth" (LS4, 94) who can share the voice of the True Law with others. They regain youthful vigor and once again begin to lead energetic lives of self-improvement. When they realize that they, too, can become Buddhas, they cry out,

> "This cluster of unsurpassed jewels
> has come to us unsought." (LS4, 87)

The "cluster of unsurpassed jewels" can be variously interpreted as indicating the teaching of the Lotus Sutra; the state of Buddhahood; or life itself, which contains within it the world of Buddhahood.

Everyone alike possesses this unsurpassed jewel of life. This most precious of all things "has come to us unsought." It comes down to whether we can recognize it as such. And the Lotus Sutra enables us to most profoundly perceive and recognize the treasure of our lives. The "unsurpassed jewel" definitely is not any material asset or "treasure of the storehouse." Someone who experienced the 1995 Great Hanshin Earthquake reportedly said: "I realized that the most important things in life are things that money can't buy: life, air and human kindness." These are words to savor.

Endo: The practitioners of the two vehicles, in their rapturous state, employ a parable to describe the teaching they have just grasped. This is the famous parable of the wealthy man and his poor son. The tale goes that the son leaves his father's house at a young age and wanders from country to country for some fifty years, growing old and poor as he does.

Saito: The wealthy father represents Shakyamuni, of course, and the poor son stands for the people of the two vehicles. The parable has traditionally been understood as referring to Shakyamuni's lifetime work of teaching and guiding others. The fifty years that the son wanders suggests the fifty years of Shakyamuni's preaching from the time he attained enlightenment at thirty to his preaching of the Lotus Sutra before his death at eighty.

Endo: When the son disappears from his father's home, the father searches but cannot find him. The father eventually takes up residence in a certain city and becomes very wealthy. His storehouses overflow with treasure, and he has countless servants and domestic animals. But the father is uneasy. He is old and knows he will die soon. He regrets that he has no heir to whom to leave his fortune and wishes to find his son and establish him as the inheritor of his wealth.

Saito: Shakyamuni has attained enlightenment, and he is looking for someone to whom he can leave all that he has attained.

Endo: One day, the son happens to pass by his father's mansion. The son is overwhelmed by the splendid mansion and the grand appearance of the man who is his father. He is afraid and begins to flee. Just then, the father recognizes his son. Though they have been separated for fifty years, the father knows his beloved son at a glance. The father sends a retainer to welcome the son home, but the son fears he is about to be apprehended for some reason and rushes away. When the retainer finally catches him, he faints in fear and exhaustion. Now the father understands that his son has fallen to such a low state that there is no use in revealing who he is just yet. So he lets the son go free.

Saito: After his enlightenment, Shakyamuni attempted to directly communicate the full content of his awakening, but his listeners were not yet ready to understand it.

Endo: The father devises a plan. He sends two poorly dressed servants to the son and offers him a job, at twice the usual wages, cleaning the father's toilets. The son works very hard. Next the father, himself dressed in poor clothes, approaches his son, speaks to and becomes acquainted with him. He says to the son:"You are a hard worker, so ask whatever you wish of me. You may think of me as your father. And I will call you 'son.'" Gradually a bond of understanding and trust grows between them, and the son comes and goes freely in the father's mansion, though he continues to live in a humble hut on its periphery.

Saito: Shakyamuni, in accordance with people's minds and their capacities, first teaches a very rudimentary teaching, leading them gradually to more and more advanced teachings. The fact that the son still lives outside his father's mansion indicates a state of mind to still regard enlightenment as something that happens to others.

Ikeda: The fact that the father tells his son to think of him as his real father is noteworthy here. In "Simile and Parable," the Buddha and living beings are said to be in a relationship of father and children. No matter what state living beings may be in, the Buddha always wishes to save them, as if they were his children. This profound relationship is key in Buddhism. Children may not understand their parents' spirit, but parents love their children, no matter how rebellious they may be. There is no parent who does not pray for his or her child's happiness.

The Buddha prays for the happiness of all beings. He fights to bring happiness to all beings. He is the parent of all beings. When we place our faith in the Buddha's intent, our own wisdom opens and blossoms. That is the meaning of "belief and understanding" in the Lotus Sutra. Voice-hearers learned of the great compassion of the Buddha, who, as their father, took great pains over many years to save his lost sons. They were greatly moved and believed and understood the Buddha's intent. That emotion is condensed into the words "belief and understanding."

Endo: Finally, the father falls sick and realizes that his end is near. He speaks to his son:

> I now have great quantities of gold, silver and rare treasures that fill and overflow from my storehouses. You are to take complete charge of the amounts I have and of what is to be handed out and gathered in. This is what I have in mind, and I want you to carry out my wishes. Why is this? Because from now on, you and I will not behave as two different persons. So you must keep your wits about you and see that there are no mistakes or losses. (LS4, 85)

The father's entire fortune is placed in the hands of the son, who manages it carefully, and who takes none of it for himself.

Saito: This corresponds to the part, "he put him in charge of household affairs" (LS4, 90). Though the father gives his son free reign in managing his wealth, the wealth remains the father's possession. The treasure of the Buddha's wisdom was still not the son's to possess as his own.

Suda: I am reminded of the passage in "On Attaining Buddhahood in this Lifetime": "If you seek enlightenment outside yourself, then your performing even ten thousand practices and ten thousand good deeds will be in vain. It is like the case of a poor man who spends night and day counting his neighbor's wealth but gains not even half a coin" (WND, 3).

Endo: Time passes, and the father realizes that his son is becoming more self-assured and magnanimous, to the point where he despises his former low opinion of himself and comes to hold high ideals. Finally, the moment of the father's death is at hand, and he calls together his relatives, the king and his ministers and says to them:

> "Gentlemen, you should know that this is my son, who was born to me. In such-and-such a city he abandoned me and ran away, and for over fifty years he wandered about suffering hardship. His original name is such-and such, and my name is such-and-such. In the past, when I was still living in my native city, I worried about him and so I set out in search of him. Sometime after, I suddenly chanced to meet up with him. This is in truth my son, and I in truth am his father. Now everything that belongs to me, all my wealth and possessions, shall belong entirely to this son of mine." (LS4, 85)

When the son learns of his true origins, he is overjoyed. "I originally had no mind to covet or seek such things," he thinks. "Yet now these stores of treasures have come of their own accord!" (LS4, 86).

Saito: When at last the son has attained a self-assured and magnanimous outlook, the father announces his true name and transfers to him all his wealth. Likewise, because the capacities of living beings had reached a high degree of development, the Buddha could expound to them the Lotus Sutra, his true teaching, bestowing upon them the supreme treasure of Buddhahood.

Suda: The Great Teacher T'ien-t'ai of China interprets this parable of the wealthy man and his poor son as explaining the fifty years of Shakyamuni's preaching. He formulates the classification of teachings known as the "five flavors," based on the process of refining ghee from milk. This schema is well known as the five periods. A particular significance (a), teaching period (b), and flavor (c) correspond to each of the five major events of the parable as follows:

1) Finding the son and pursuing him:
    (a) testing the people's capacities
    (b) Flower Garland period
    (c) milk

2) Inviting the son to work in his mansion:
    (a) leading in the right direction
    (b) Agana period
    (c) cream

3) Forging bonds of trust between father and son:
    (a) refuting adherence to the Theravada teaching
    (b) Correct and Equal period
    (c) curdled milk

4) Turning management of the estate over to the son:
    (a) eliminating nonessentials
    (b) Wisdom period
    (c) butter

5) Officially leaving the wealth to the son:
    (a) opening and unifying
    (b) Lotus period
    (c) ghee

Endo: The Lotus Sutra is the ghee, the most refined, of all the Buddha's teachings. One cannot know how truly "delicious"

Buddhism is without savoring the Lotus Sutra. Shakyamuni first revealed a kind of rough sketch of the world of his enlightenment (in the Flower Garland Sutra), but it was completely beyond the comprehension of the practitioners of the two vehicles. So Shakyamuni taught the Agon Sutras, in accord with the low aspirations of his listeners; he set up the lowly goals of the Theravada teachings. Next he taught the Mahayana sutras for those with higher aims. But the practitioners of the two vehicles clung to the Theravada teachings and showed no interest in the Mahayana teachings.

Saito: The practitioners of the two vehicles later reflect on their behavior at that time and describe it as "being satisfied with a day's wages and not seeking to earn more."

Ikeda: While in general it is important "to desire little and be content with what one has," it is good to be greedy for the True Law. The goal is not to eliminate desires; it is what one desires that is important. Earthly desires are enlightenment. The desire for supreme enlightenment, the search for enlightenment, is enlightenment. Satisfaction with one's accomplishments might seem like humility, but to underestimate life's potential is actually great arrogance.

Endo: The practitioners of the two vehicles cling to the minor teachings of the Theravada and have no interest in the Mahayana teachings, so Shakyamuni firmly reprimands them. In "Belief and Understanding," the four great men of Learning reflect: "In the past, when in the presence of the bodhisattvas he disparaged the voice-hearers as those who delight in a lesser doctrine, the Buddha was in fact employing the Great Vehicle to teach and convert us" (LS4, 87). Here "Great Vehicle" refers to the one and only true Mahayana teaching, namely, the Lotus Sutra. This is the true wealth of the Buddha.

The Meaning of "Belief and Understanding"

Suda: "Belief and Understanding" describes how the voice-hearers believe and understand the Buddha's teaching and rejoice at being able to do so. That is why the chapter is titled "Belief and Understanding." The Sanskrit for "belief and understanding" is *adhimukti,* which literally means inclination or intent, that is, to direct one's mind or will toward something. Since it involves direction of the mind, I think we could also call it an aim or a purpose. *Mukti* is thought to be related to the Sanskrit word for liberation, *moksha.* Given that context, I think Kumarajiva's translation of the chapter title in the Myoho-renge-kyo as "belief and understanding" is a deeper interpretation than the Dharmaraksha's translation of the title in his Sho-hokke-kyo[4] as "belief and delight."

Ikeda: In the "Record of the Oral Teachings," Nichiren Daishonin quotes Miao-lo's *Annotations on the "Words and Phrases of the Lotus Sutra"*: "In the Sho-hokke-kyo, this chapter ['Belief and Understanding'] is titled 'Belief and Delight.' While both have a similar meaning, the word *delight* is less appropriate than *understanding.* The chapter describes how the four great men of Learning gain an understanding of the teachings, but what justification is there for the use of the word *delight*?" (GZ, 725).

The important point is that the fundamental issues for Buddhism of faith and wisdom, and faith and liberation (enlightenment) are distilled in "belief and understanding." In a broader sense, this relates to the fundamental issues of civilization and philosophy, which are faith and reason, believing and knowing. This is an extremely delicate problem, with relevance to many disciplines, including the cognitive sciences and psychology. Buddhism has traditionally considered these issues in meticulous detail.

Of course, we can hardly do this matter justice in a single meeting, but neither can we avoid it entirely. The philosopher Blaise Pascal writes, "We must declare that religion is not irrational."[5]

These words, directed toward people without religious faith, remain alive today. Many today regard any kind of belief—and religious faith, in particular—as somehow in opposition to reason or at the very least as a sort of paralysis of the faculty of reason. There are, indeed, fanatical religions in which faith opposes reason. But it is an erroneous leap of logic to assume on this basis, and without any evidence, that all religions are so. That itself is irrational and can be characterized as a kind of blind faith in its own right.

A higher religion does not negate rationality. No religion that suppresses human reason can earn the trust of humankind. Buddhism, the "religion of wisdom," is an extremely rational religion. In fact, it is so rational that many Westerners even question whether it can be classified as a religion, since it does not teach the existence of a supreme being in the image of humankind.

Suda: A tendency toward rationalism seems especially strong in early Buddhism. In Mahayana Buddhism, however, there is strong emphasis on faith.

Ikeda: Yes, that's true, but even in early Buddhism, practice is based on faith in Shakyamuni, and faith in the Buddha's teachings is also encouraged. Faith was the starting point for the intellectual quest. Moreover, the basis in faith made possible a kind of intellectual quest involving one's entire being, including intuitive powers of perception and the deepest levels of awareness, rather than merely analytical intelligence.

Saito: It is certainly true that faith in one's teacher is necessary for success in any kind of discipline or training, not only religion. Mr. Makiguchi said: "We learn how to live by imitating others. We observe what others do and copy what we see, trusting in their example. The same is true of flower arrangement, dance, kendo, judo or any other art or skill. We trust our teachers and do what they say. After mastering imitation, we move on to creativity. That is how one learns to live."[6]

Endo: If a newborn infant were not to believe what its parents taught it—if it thought milk was poison, if it refused to drink water—it would not survive. The first step in life is belief; everything develops from that. No society can exist without bonds of mutual trust among its members.

Ikeda: That's true. This belief on the level of daily life is, of course, different from religious faith, but neither are they utterly divorced from each other. They are part of a shared continuum. The Spanish philosopher José Ortega y Gasset writes, "We have ideas, but we live based on our beliefs."[7] Even when we have an idea, that is, when we think, we still base our thoughts on beliefs we hold. Beliefs are the "vessel" of life.

Ortega continues: "Our beliefs are already operating in the depths of our lives when we begin to think about something."[8]

"Our beliefs constitute the basis of our lives, the ground on which human life unfolds.... All our behavior, including our intellectual activities, depends on our system of authentic beliefs. We live, act and exist within our beliefs. For precisely that reason, we do not have a very clear perception of our beliefs, and we usually do not think about them. Yet those beliefs, operating in a latent fashion, are a part of all our conscious acts and thoughts."[9]

Ortega describes belief as "the foundation of knowledge." If we accept Ortega's position, we can see that the conflict between knowledge and belief now commonly thought to exist is by no means self-evident. Belief is the foundation of life, and as such we don't really have a choice to believe or not. We can choose, however, what we will believe in. Religions are systematic presentations of things that should and should not be believed. In that respect, religion is an indispensable part of the life of every individual, and it plays a crucial part in each day of our lives.

Suda: Most people are simply not well aware of the beliefs upon which they base their lives.

Saito: As Ortega might say, the more completely we are living within our beliefs, the less we are conscious of them. As long as that is the case, there is little chance that we can consider the correctness of our beliefs rationally. In that sense, those who think themselves most completely without beliefs—who "believe that they have no beliefs"—are in fact the most irrational about the beliefs on which their lives are based.

Ikeda: We can liken this "ground" of belief to the earth. We are usually unaware of the earth upon which we walk; but we are keenly aware of it when an earthquake occurs. Likewise, we are never more aware of our beliefs than when they crumble. On the individual level, this occurs when we find ourselves in a desperate situation that forces us to reevaluate how we have lived up to then.

Most of those who gathered around Shakyamuni came to him seeking a new realm of belief after they had experienced such frustration and suffering. On a cultural level, this occurs when a civilization reaches a dead end and its basic underlying values are called into question. We are without a doubt living in such an age today. In particular, in connection with the issue of "belief and understanding," the presumption of a sharp division and opposition between belief on the one hand, and understanding or knowledge on the other, which has been a hallmark of contemporary thought, is being reexamined. In its place, a new fusion of belief and knowledge is being sought.

Endo: I am reminded of a speech you gave at Soka University titled "Scholastic Philosophy and Modern Civilization" (in July 1973). You presented Scholasticism, which has been widely regarded as the "official philosophy" of the Middle Ages, in a new light. You suggested that it could contribute greatly to the issues of unifying belief and reason and developing a holistic knowledge.

Suda: The view of reason as a function independent of all else seems to be losing ground. In the history of science, for example, there is much talk of a paradigm shift. Until recently, scientific knowledge has been regarded as universal, objective and unchanging from age to age. But now it is recognized that such knowledge is inseparable from the intellectual paradigms—the ways of thinking and value systems—that dominated the ages in which the scientists lived.

Endo: There is increasing recognition that reason is ultimately founded on belief. Many thinkers now accept the view that reason is always based on the paradigms that people, including scientists, believe and accept and upon which they base their lives.

Saito: Modern scientists have discussed this point from a variety of angles. Ludwig Wittgenstein, the Austrian philosopher who has exerted great influence on contemporary thought, insisted that all knowledge rests on the thinker's worldview. In other words, our lives are rooted in an undemonstrable system of belief, apart from which reason cannot operate. Thus, even the skeptic, who claims to believe in nothing and who questions all, in fact believes in skepticism.

Suda: The German philosopher Hans-Georg Gadamer holds that human experience is ultimately defined by history. We cannot create an identity separate from the society in which we were born and raised. Every individual starts out from the beliefs that his or her society sanctions.

Ikeda: Each person's life is based on belief of some kind, and therefore such beliefs should be duly respected. But unless that belief is subjected to the tests of reason and reality, it remains individual and subjective and lacks the universality to be communicated to others. The fact that the belief taught in the Lotus Sutra is one with understanding indicates that it is not simply subjective or arbitrary. Of course, the fundamental law to which the Buddha is enlightened is beyond description, meaning that it cannot be grasped in its entirety with language or reason. Even so, Buddhism teaches that reason and language should be highly valued albeit with recognition of their limitations. While the Buddha's enlightenment may be beyond the realm of reason, it is not irrational, nor does it resist rational examination. *Understanding*, as in "belief and understanding," means wisdom. This wisdom is not reason itself but works in conjunction with reason, and reason is a part of it. It is reasonable to the highest degree, and at the same time it is holistic wisdom that transcends reason. Practicing "belief and understanding" means acquiring that highest wisdom through faith.

Endo: Nichiren Daishonin also practiced this highest teaching of Buddhism, which is supremely rational. For example, he frequently confirms his own position by first presenting various doubts and then refuting them. So it was that before proclaiming the establishment of his teaching, he visited temples all over Japan. He writes that he had doubts about the Buddhism of his day, which was divided into various schools: "Yet the ten schools and seven schools I have mentioned all argue with one another over which of the sutras it is [that is supreme] and can reach no consensus. It is as though seven men or ten men were all trying to be the monarch of a single nation, thus keeping the populace in constant turmoil. Wondering how to resolve this dilemma, I made a vow. I decided that I would not heed the claims of these eight or ten schools…" (WND, 691–92).

The Daishonin did not submit blindly to the authorities of his day. He thought for himself, based on the scriptures, and sought proof to substantiate his beliefs.

Saito: The same was true during his exile to Sado Island. Responding to the question, raised by his followers as well as by others, as to why the votary of the Lotus Sutra should be persecuted, he replies in "The Opening of the Eyes": "This doubt lies at the heart of this piece I am writing. And because it is the most important concern of my entire life, I will raise it again and again here, and emphasize it more than ever, before I attempt to answer it" (WND, 243).

The Daishonin addresses the question head on and through considering it rationally comes to the conclusion that he is the Buddha of the Latter Day of the Law. The Daishonin's faith welcomes questions. Through questions, it arrives at answers on a higher level. In this, we see that the Daishonin's faith was always open to intellectual criticism.

Ikeda: There is a famous passage in "The Opening of the Eyes": "Whatever obstacles I might encounter, so long as persons of wisdom do not prove my teachings to be false, I will never yield! All other troubles are no more to me than dust before the wind" (WND, 280). This expresses the Daishonin's conviction that his teachings could not be destroyed by any kind of criticism and also shows us how much he valued the intellect. Finally, in "The True Aspect of All Phenomena," he emphasizes the importance of study, along with practice: "Exert yourself in the two ways of practice and study. Without practice and study, there can be no Buddhism" (WND, 386). The Daishonin declares that without the pursuit of knowledge, without the test of reason, there is no Buddhism.

SUBSTITUTING FAITH FOR WISDOM

Suda: To return to the Lotus Sutra, we find two Sanskrit words that are often translated as faith or belief. In addition to *adhimukti,* or "belief and understanding," the sutra also uses the term *sraddha.* The root meaning of *dha* of *sraddha* is "to place," so *sraddha* means "to place one's faith" or "to arouse faith." This is defined as the first stage of Buddhist practice. In the ancient Hindu scriptures called the Vedas, which predate the Buddhist scriptures, *sraddha* is used to mean "to possess curiosity about" or "to yearn for." It has been said that a feeling of astonishment is the source of religious sentiment. *Sraddha* includes the meanings of awe and yearning for the object of that astonishment. It is a feeling of reverent wonder, or piety, toward that which is beyond one's ken. Whoever lacks such a sense of piety and is governed instead by passions and desires is called in Buddhist texts an *icchantika*, a person of incorrigible disbelief and neither has faith in Buddhism nor aspires for enlightenment.

Saito: Buddhist practice begins by arousing *sraddha.* Then, as our practice progresses, we acquire wisdom from experiencing that which was formerly inconceivable, and we proceed toward enlightenment and its benefit.

Endo: That's why in the Flower Garland Sutra *sraddha* is described as the "basis of practice" and "mother of blessings." "Faith," in the Lotus Sutra's principle of substituting faith for wisdom, is *sraddha.* Nichiren Daishonin writes, "To have faith is the basis of Buddhism" (WND, 832).

Ikeda: Faith in Buddhism is definitely not fanaticism or blind faith that rejects the criteria of reason. It is in fact a rational function, a process of cultivating wisdom that begins with a spirit of reverent searching.

Saito: There is yet another Buddhist term for faith: *prasada. Prasada* expresses the idea of purity and clarity, as in a clear voice or pure water. It is used to describe the pure state of mind of those whose confusion has been dispelled by hearing the teachings of Buddhism. It is translated into Chinese by two characters meaning "pure faith." The state of pure faith is one in which we are always at peace, never disturbed by any circumstance, and realize the dignity and equality of all living things.

Ikeda: The proper function of faith is to cleanse the mind and make it pure. Only when the mind is pure can our inherent wisdom shine forth. Some philosophers have considered reason the "slave of the passions" and believed that reason needed to be freed from the "pollution" of emotion. Others, such as Saint Augustine (an early Christian philosopher), held that faith was needed to cure and strengthen "ailing reason." What these many different positions have in common is the belief that reason must not be allowed to degenerate into a self-satisfied arrogance.

The impulse of true reason is to continuously and eternally transcend the confines of the present self. It aims to reach beyond its grasp, always improving, always surpassing itself. The source of energy and foundation for that constant search is faith in something larger than oneself. Faith purifies reason, strengthens it, and elevates it. "Pure faith" is at once thoroughly polished faith and rigorously tested reason.

Suda: In "Expedient Means," Shariputra entreats Shakyamuni: "Speak, we beg you, without reserve! / In this assembly of numberless beings / are those capable of reverent belief" (LS2, 29). The "reverent belief" to which Shariputra attests is faith that encompasses both *sraddha* and *prasada*.

Endo: I think we can summarize the three kinds of faith as follows. When we first hear the Buddhist teachings, we feel a wonderful awe and, arousing "reverent faith" (*sraddha*), we commence our Buddhist practice. Through developing "belief and understanding" (*adhimukti*), we cultivate and polish our lives toward perfecting the sublime state that is pure faith (*prasada*), by which one perceives that all living beings are equal and have dignity.

Ikeda: Buddhist faith is the engine for continuous self-improvement. It is a force that motivates us to strive for the perfection of our entire being, including the intellect, and to develop our hidden potential to the fullest.

Suda: There is yet another kind of faith, which is called *bhakti* in Sanskrit. This is a burning and absolute faith in a deity. The original meaning of *bhakti* is to "share" or "become a part of." *Bhakti* is used, for example, to refer to becoming one with Brahma, which the Hindu religion holds to be the origin of, and to encompass, all beings. It is a faith that leads to unification with some mystical being that transcends the individual, and it leads to a practice in which one surrenders his or her identity to some greater being. *Bhakti* is used frequently in Indian texts to refer to absolute faith in a deity, but it is almost never used in Buddhist texts. *Bhakti* is an essentially different kind of faith from that espoused in Buddhism.

Ikeda: That's true. Buddhism does not teach self-negation toward being subsumed in some larger entity. Our individual lives are each infinite treasure houses. Our lives are clusters of blessings. Our lives are the Lotus Sutra. Lasting happiness never comes from the outside. Everything of value emanates from within our own being. Faith in Buddhism means establishing one's true self. It is the recognition that the infinite horizon of the cosmos exists right here within the self. One's life opens out toward the cosmos and is enfolded in it; at the same time, one's life encompasses the entire cosmos. We are in constant exchange and communication with the cosmos, our lives reverberating with it as one living entity. Faith is the "springboard" for attaining that awareness.

Endo: I think we have to take up the question of why the Lotus Sutra emphasizes faith so much more than do other Buddhist texts.

Saito: Faith is already strongly emphasized at the very start of Shakyamuni's preaching in "Expedient Means." After the true entity of all phenomena and the ten factors of life are presented, Shariputra asks Shakyamuni to preach the teaching that has never been taught before.

Shakyamuni replies that if he does so, people will be astonished and will doubt the teaching, and three times he refuses Shariputra's request. But Shariputra vows, "The countless members of this assembly / are capable of according reverent belief to this Law" (LS2, 30), and once again requests that Shakyamuni teach it.

In response to Shariputra's strong and reverent faith, Shakyamuni reveals that the reason the Buddha appears in the world is "to open the door of the Buddha wisdom," "to show the Buddha wisdom," "to awaken [all beings] to the Buddha wisdom," and "to induce [them] to enter the path of the Buddha wisdom" (LS2, 31). And he begins to expound the replacement of the three vehicles with the one supreme vehicle.

Ikeda: As we see from this, faith is a prerequisite for the very preaching of the Lotus Sutra.

Endo: Shariputra, the first of the men of Learning to hear the Buddha's teaching in the "Expedient Means" chapter and attain enlightenment, does so not by the power of his own wisdom but through faith—by substituting faith for wisdom.

As *The Treatise on the Great Perfection of Wisdom*[10] explains, "It is faith through which one enters the sea of Buddhism, and wisdom by which one crosses it." Buddhist practice starts from faith. That leads to the acquisition of wisdom, and the power of wisdom carries us across the great sea of Buddhism—that is, to supreme enlightenment. This is the general outlook of Buddhism.

But the Lotus Sutra emphasizes attaining enlightenment through faith rather than through wisdom. Indeed, faith is substituted for wisdom in the sutra.

Ikeda: This is very significant. The Lotus Sutra is like all of the Buddhist teachings in that wisdom equals Buddhahood. But in the Lotus Sutra, wisdom is inherent in faith. That is the significance of "belief and understanding." Nichiren Daishonin writes,

"Understanding is another name for wisdom," and "There is no understanding separate from faith and no faith separate from understanding" (GZ, 725). "Understanding" (*ge*) here is part of the word for "liberation" (*gedatsu*), in the sense of enlightenment. It is a state of liberation and total freedom from all suffering, and it is a state of wisdom that can only be attained through faith.

Endo: The Lotus Sutra emphasizes "a single moment of belief and understanding." In "Distinctions in Benefits," the seventeenth chapter, we find: "If there are living beings who, on hearing that the life span of the Buddha is of such long duration, are able to believe and understand it even for a moment, the benefits they gain thereby will be without limit or measure" (LS17, 237). The sutra continues, "If after the Thus Come One has entered extinction there are those who hear this sutra and do not slander or speak ill of it but feel joy in their hearts, you should know that this is a sign that they have already shown deep faith and understanding" (LS17, 240).

Those who rejoice when they hear the Mystic Law do so because they have already attained deep belief and understanding, according to the sutra. We can interpret this to mean that the essence of Buddhahood lies in belief and understanding.

Ikeda: I am sure we will discuss this in greater depth when we take up "Distinctions in Benefits," but the essence of the Lotus Sutra is to be found in the first of both the four stages of faith and the five stages of practice. These are the stages of "producing even a single moment of belief and understanding in the sutra" and "rejoicing on hearing the Lotus Sutra."

Suda: Isn't the key to the emphasis on faith in the Lotus Sutra the fact that it was taught according to the Buddha's own mind?

Ikeda: Precisely. Sutras had been expounded to match the capacities of listeners, meaning that they were easier to grasp. They were easy to believe and easy to understand. But the world of Buddha-hood, transcending people's powers of thought and imagination, is difficult to believe and difficult to understand. That is why faith is emphasized.

Discussing the differences between the Lotus Sutra and all other sutras of past, present and future, Nichiren Daishonin quotes a passage from the Great Teacher Dengyo's *The Outstanding Principles of the Lotus Sutra*: "All the sutras of the first four (of the five) periods preached in the past, the Immeasurable Meanings Sutra now being preached, and the Nirvana Sutra to be preached in the future are easy to believe and easy to understand. This is because the Buddha taught these sutras in accordance with the capacity of his listeners. The Lotus Sutra is the most difficult to believe and to understand because in it the Buddha directly revealed what he had attained" (WND, 1037).

The sutra taught in accordance with the Buddha's own intent far surpasses ordinary people's powers of understanding; it is beyond our intellectual grasp. Only through belief and understanding can we gain access to it.

The secret of the Mystic Law, which enables us to enjoy a state of absolute freedom at one with the universe, is beyond our ordinary comprehension, just as a rocket would be beyond the ability of someone who has no experience of such technology to comprehend it. That is why the only way to enter the path of the Mystic Law is through the power of strong faith.

But I am not speaking of blind faith. It is faith based on documentary, theoretical and actual proof. As Tsunesaburo Makiguchi said:

> Though we may lack advanced medical knowledge ourselves, that does not stop us from trusting in a doctor and allowing him to treat our illness. When we do so, we look, consciously or not, for a doctor who meets the following three conditions:

(1) He or she must be a doctor with documentary proof of training and ability. We look for a diploma, a title and a record of work in a field of specialization.

(2) Next we look for a doctor who has successfully treated a large number of people, that is, the actual proof of ability.

(3) Finally, if the doctor's method of treatment is reasonable from a medical perspective, all our doubts are put to rest. This is what we call reason, or theoretical proof.[11]

Endo: So even on this level of daily life, the principle of substituting faith for wisdom applies, as do the three kinds of proof. Buddhism indeed encompasses all phenomena.

Ikeda: The reason the Lotus Sutra emphasizes faith or belief so strongly is that the goal of the sutra is to eliminate the fundamental ignorance of life, what Buddhism calls "fundamental darkness," and to cause all beings to awaken to their "fundamental enlightenment," the wisdom originally inherent in the lives of each. This "fundamental enlightenment" can also be described as the Buddha nature or the world of Buddhahood.

But this fundamental enlightenment exists at a level so deep within our being that the intellect or reason, which operates more on life's surface, is unable to reveal it in its entirety.

Only when we open our entire being, including our intellectual faculties, to the Mystic Law does the Buddha nature, the world of Buddhahood, manifest in our lives.

Nichiren Daishonin writes, "Faith is a sharp sword which cuts the fundamental darkness of life" (GZ, 725). Faith opens; doubt closes. When we open ourselves to the Mystic Law, the Mystic Law in turn opens to us. That is the meaning of Nichikan's statement that "Strong faith in the Lotus Sutra is itself Buddhahood."

The ultimate law of the universe is too vast to be grasped fully by the human mind, which is but a tiny part of that universe. But we can develop ourselves so that the Mystic Law becomes manifest in our lives. That is the purpose of faith in and devotion to the Mystic Law. The Daishonin writes, "Belief corresponds to the eternal and unchanging truth.... Understanding corresponds to its functions in accordance with changing circumstances" (GZ, 725).

Through believing in and devoting ourselves to the Mystic Law, the Mystic Law becomes manifest in our lives, and our lives will accord with the Law. The "proof" of vibrant life force that we attain through faith in the Mystic Law represents the wisdom that "functions in accordance with changing circumstances," or the understanding of "belief and understanding."

The Daishonin also says: "Belief represents the value or price we attach to a jewel or treasure, and understanding represents the jewel itself. It is through belief that we can 'purchase' the wisdom of the Buddhas of past, present and future" (GZ, 725).

In that regard, belief and understanding are far from opposites, nor is belief something static that is enlisted in support of understanding. In fact, they are essentially one. If we try to separate them, we can only describe them as partners in a dynamic cycle in which belief leads to understanding and understanding further strengthens belief. Through this unending cycle, we can continuously cultivate and improve ourselves. This is the fundamental meaning of "belief and understanding."

It is interesting that the Sanskrit *adhimukti* can also be translated as "will" or "intent." Buddhahood is not a static state. The true state of the Buddha's life is one of endlessly seeking self-improvement, in which wisdom deepens compassion and compassion deepens wisdom. It is a process of boundlessly and continuously striving for perfection. The two wheels of that will to perfection, which carry it along on its eternal journey, are faith and understanding.

Saito: In contemporary society, faith is viewed as an intellectual crutch that paralyzes reason and causes one to dwell in a closed, subjective world. But now I see that this is not at all the meaning of faith and understanding in the Lotus Sutra.

Ikeda: That's correct. The belief taught in the Lotus Sutra provides no easy answers, no escape route from the difficulties of human life. In fact, it rejects such easy answers; instead it implores us to take up the two tools for exploring life, belief and understanding, and use them to continually challenge and work to perfect ourselves. And it also provides us the energy to do just that.

The modern age maintains the illusion that intellect is an independent faculty, divorced from belief. Yet aren't we now seeing that in fact many so-called modern notions, such as materialism, actually rest on beliefs, or premises, that are entirely unexamined? And actions based thereon have been the source of much suffering and turmoil.

What is called for now is a new unification of belief and reason encompassing all aspects of the human being and society, including the perspective achieved by modern science. This is the great challenge that modern civilization faces. It is an attempt to restore the wholeness of human society, which has been rent asunder by reason without belief and irrational fanaticism.

It might be construed as the story of the wandering son — modern rationality — returning to his parental home — life itself.

This unification of belief and understanding will be the key to getting modern society back on course from its spiritual drift and helping humankind attain the summit of life's true promise.

NOTES

1. Kumarajiva (344–413): translator of the Lotus Sutra into Chinese.

2. Translated from the Japanese: *Hokekyo jo* (The Lotus Sutra, vol. 1), trans. Yukio Sakamoto and Yutaka Iwamoto (Tokyo: Iwanami Shoten, 1962), pp. 233–25.

3. Ibid., *Hokekyo jo*, p. 225.

4. The Japanese transliterated title of the earliest Chinese translation of the Saddharamapundarika-sutra, consisting of twenty-seven chapters in ten volumes. This translation (dated 286) corresponds with the Myoho-renge-kyo (406) of Kumarajiva in most respects, except that it contains several parables, which the latter omits.

5. Translated from the Japanese: Blaise Pascal, *Panse* (Pansee), trans. Yoichi Maeda and Ko Yuuki, in *Seikai no meicho* 24 (World Masterpieces, vol. 24) (Tokyo: Chuokoronsha, 1996), p. 141.

6. *Makiguchi Tsunesaburo Shingenshu* (Collection of Tsunesaburo Makiguchi's Sayings), ed. Takeshi Tsuji (Tokyo: Daisan Bunmei Publishing Co., 1979), pp. 16–17.

7. José Ortega y Gasset, *Ideas y Creencias (y Otros Ensayos de Filosofia)* (Madrid: Alianaza Editorial, 1986), p. 23.

8. Ibid., p. 26.

9. Ibid., p. 29.

10. *Treatise on the Sutra of the Perfection of Wisdom*, one of Nagarjuna's writings.

11. *Makiguchi Tsunesaburo Shingenshu*, p. 19.

PART THREE

"The Parable of the Medicinal Herbs" Chapter

3   The Buddha's Compassionate Wisdom
Fosters Individuality

Saito: In her book, *The Future: Images and Processes,* Elise Boulding quotes children ages ten through fourteen about their vision of the world in 2005 (which coincidentally is the seventy-fifth anniversary of the Soka Gakkai). These interviews all took place about twenty years ago!

Ikeda: What will the world be like in 2005? One child describes his vision of the world:

> This is the year 2005 and the Earth is green and fertile on one side of the Earth, and the other side is black smoke and all polluted. Nothing can grow on that side of the world. On the green side of the Earth, kids are playing all day and all night. We never sleep. On the black side there are just robots wishing that they could play. There is a wall separating the black side and the green side of the Earth. The wall is called the wall of justice. It keeps the pollution on the black side of the Earth.... Scientists say that in ten years we will have to build a new wall of justice or move to the moon.[1]

Another child writes: "I think in the year 2005 we...will be at war and some of the government will be different. They will try to run our lives, tell us who to marry and what job to get. Men will be doing the housework and cooking and the women will come home from work and sit down in their favorite chair [to watch television]."[2]

And another says: "I would like the people to be kind.... There would be no guns, and there would not be any wars. We would be friendly with the Martians."[3]

Endo: Elise Boulding is a world-class scholar known for her research in a wide range of areas, including peace studies, education and women's issues. She was also named the first recipient of the Global Citizen Award by the Boston Research Center for the 21st Century in 1995.

Suda: The Future was co-authored by her late husband, Kenneth Boulding, who was a prominent economist and a pioneer of peace studies.

Saito: I sense that in publishing the Bouldings' book, their purpose was not to blithely report the words of children but to sound a warning for adult society.

Endo: That's right. Children, in their own way, are thinking about the future of the planet. And because they can sense more readily what is good or bad, they are probably in a position to see things with originality and freshness beyond the reach of adults.

Ikeda: Elise Boulding, who conducted the interviews in the book, has asserted all along that children must be co-participants in the building of future society. If we can create a social environment that responds to children's hopes, she reasons, it will probably also afford a richness of life for adults.

She emphatically sums up her position: "We must take control of our lives, because within us is the seed of a new reality—a seed that cannot grow until our lives are our own. It is a reality of ecstasy, made up of love, justice, freedom, peace, and plenty."[4]

She describes a yearning to open the "seed of joy" in the lives of all people. The Lotus Sutra explains that all people can open up the unsurpassed seed of the Buddha nature in their lives. And "The Parable of the Medicinal Herbs," the fifth chapter, describes the Buddha's undiscriminating compassion that makes this possible.

THE PARABLE OF THE THREE KINDS OF MEDICINAL HERBS AND TWO KINDS OF TREES

> The equality of the Buddha's preaching
> is like a rain of a single flavor,
> but depending upon the nature of the living being,
> the way in which it is received is not uniform,
> just as the various plants and trees
> each receive the moisture in a different manner.
> The Buddha employs this parable
> as an expedient means to open up and reveal the matter,
> using various kinds of words and phrases
> and expounding the single Law,
> but in terms of the Buddha wisdom
> this is no more than one drop of the ocean.
> I rain down the Dharma rain,
> filling the whole world,
> and this single-flavored Dharma
> is practiced by each according to the individual's power.
> It is like those thickets and groves,
> medicinal herbs and trees
> which, according to whether they are large or small,
> bit by bit grow lush and beautiful. (LS5, 104)

Saito: I'd like to start by explaining the position of the "Medicinal Herbs" chapter within the Lotus Sutra.

In the fourth chapter, "Belief and Understanding," Kashyapa[5] and the other great voice-hearers[6] indicate that they understand

Shakyamuni's preaching [of the parable of the three carts and the burning house[7] in "Simile and Parable," the third chapter] by relating the parable of the wealthy man and his poor son.

In "Medicinal Herbs," Shakyamuni, having heard this discourse, praises the four great voice-hearers, saying: "Excellent, excellent, Kashyapa. You have given an excellent description of the true blessings of the Thus Come One" (LS5, 97). He further states: "The Thus Come One indeed has immeasurable, boundless, asamkhyas of blessings, and though you and the others were to spend immeasurable millions of kalpas in the effort, you could never finish describing them" (LS5, 97). Shakyamuni then expounds the parable of the three kinds of medicinal herbs and two kinds of trees.

"Medicinal Herbs" thus serves a twofold purpose. In it, the Buddha both affirms the earlier teaching his disciples have grasped and supplements it with an additional teaching. The Great Teacher T'ien-t'ai of China designates this manner of preaching as "presentation and mastery."[8]

Then, in "Bestowal of Prophecy," the next chapter, each of the four great voice-hearers is given a prophecy that he is certain to become a Buddha. Shakyamuni specifically indicates when, where and under what name each will attain enlightenment.

Endo: In other words, we see a four-step development: Shakyamuni's initial preaching, understanding by the four great voice-hearers, Shakyamuni's affirmation and additional preaching (presentation and mastery), and the prophecy of enlightenment for the four.

We see the same four-step process in the cases of both Shariputra (in "Expedient Means," the second chapter) and the group of voice-hearers represented by Purna[9] (in "The Parable of the Phantom City," the seventh chapter).

Ikeda: This life-to-life exchange, this oneness of mentor and disciple holds the key to attaining Buddhahood.

Leaving the discussion of the prophecy of enlightenment for another occasion, we can say that Shakyamuni, in employing "presentation and mastery," seeks to clarify that the voice-hearers who believe and understand his Lotus Sutra preaching have undoubtedly entered the bodhisattva path leading to Buddha-hood.

Saito: This is clearly indicated at the close of "Medicinal Herbs" where Shakyamuni says:

> What you are practicing
> is the bodhisattva way,
> and as you gradually advance in practice and learning
> you are all certain to attain Buddhahood. (LS5, 106)

Endo: And it is on this premise that Shakyamuni later prophesies enlightenment for each of the voice-hearers.

Ikeda: To unfailingly enter the path to enlightenment is the ben-efit of believing and understanding the one Buddha vehicle of the Lotus Sutra. The parable in "Medicinal Herbs" of the three kinds of medicinal herbs and two kinds of trees explains this ben-efit in further detail.

Suda: Let me try to summarize the parable.

First, it is pointed out that various trees and medicinal herbs grow in mountains and streams, ravines and valleys throughout the world, and that these plants differ in name and form. Of these grasses and trees, the medicinal herbs are distinguished as superior, middling or inferior, and the trees as large or small. That's why it is called the parable of the three kinds of medicinal herbs and two kinds of trees.

It says: "A great cloud...rises up in the world and covers it all over. This beneficent cloud is laden with moisture" (LS5, 100–01). The rain from this cloud falls widely, moistening the trees and medicinal herbs. And while the rain falls everywhere equally, the medicinal herbs and trees grow according to their respective natures and produce different flowers and fruit.

The parable explains that there are many distinctions among the multitude of herbs and trees, even though they grow in the same earth and are moistened by the same rain.

Endo: The "great cloud" represents the Buddha, and its rising up and covering the world signifies the Buddha's appearance. Also, the rain that falls equally everywhere represents the Buddha's preaching and is called "Dharma rain." The various plants and trees are the various living beings, and their receiving the rainfall signifies "hearing the Law." Also, the growth and the production of flowers and fruit by the plants and trees could be said to correspond to practice and benefit.

Of the three kinds of medicinal herbs, the inferior medicinal herbs stand for those beings in the worlds of Humanity and Heaven. The middling herbs represent those in the worlds of Learning and Realization. And the superior herbs and the two kinds of trees, small and large, all indicate those in the world of Bodhisattva who aspire to become Buddhas.

Suda: Given that the superior medicinal herbs and the small and large trees all represent bodhisattvas, the question arises as to how these should be further distinguished. Over the ages a variety of theories have been proposed. T'ien-t'ai, for example, says that the superior herbs correspond to bodhisattvas of the Tripitaka (or Theravada) teaching; the small trees to those of the connecting (or introductory Mahayana) teaching; and the large trees to those of the specific teaching (so called because it was expounded specifically for bodhisattvas).

Saito: That the rain falls equally signifies that the Law the Buddha preaches is "of one form, one flavor" (LS5, 99). This means that ultimately the Buddha's preaching contains the benefit to enable all people equally to become Buddhas; it is the one Buddha vehicle.

Ikeda: That's the essence of the Buddha's preaching from the Buddha's standpoint. But the people, for their part, fail to understand this benefit. The quantity of the rain received and its efficacy differ according to the particular character and size of the plants and trees. Similarly, although the Buddha expounds only the one Buddha vehicle, there are differences in how people receive this teaching. As it filters down through people's understanding, the Buddha's teaching takes on the form of the so-called three vehicles.

Suda: Ultimately, the parable of the three kinds of medicinal herbs and two kinds of trees, like the preceding two parables (of the three carts and the burning house, and of the wealthy man and his poor son), expresses the principle of the replacement of the three vehicles with the one vehicle.

For one thing, it clarifies (as do these earlier parables) why the Buddha has expounded the teachings of the three vehicles. It indicates that because people differ widely in terms of their intellectual capacity and disposition to receive the Buddha's teachings, the Buddha expounded a variety of teachings to match the capacity and tendency of each.

Also, this parable clarifies that while the Buddha's teachings are many and varied, their essence in every case is the one Buddha vehicle. And, like the rain, it falls upon all equally and has one "flavor."

Ikeda: I am always impressed by the marvelous skill of the parables in the Lotus Sutra. The Chinese author Jin Yong[10], with whom I have spoken, characterizes the Lotus Sutra as a "record of dialogue" between Shakyamuni and his disciples and as "great literature" for its skillful use of metaphor.

Suda: I gather that he has a keen interest in Buddhism, and in the Lotus Sutra in particular.

Ikeda: He knows a great deal about Buddhism. One of his novels, *Semi-Gods and Semi-Devils*, takes its original Chinese title from a line in the "Devadatta" chapter of the Lotus Sutra. The beings thus indicated—including heavenly beings, dragons and *yakshas*—are among the assembly gathered in the sutra's "Introduction" chapter.

Endo: Collectively, these are known as the eight kinds of nonhuman beings.

Ikeda: That's right. The novel is set in a Buddhist land called Dali during China's Northern Sung period (960–1127). The expression "semi-gods and semi-devils" in the title reflects the diverse personalities of the characters.

Suda: You proposed that he write the calligraphy for the Hiroshima Prayer for Peace Monument.[11]

Ikeda: He is a fighter wielding the pen of peace who has consistently and forcefully argued against nuclear weapons. After careful consideration, I concluded that Jin Yong would be the most suitable person to pen the inscription.

I understand that since then he has been reading the Lotus Sutra and practicing his hand every day. Because, as he put it, he wants to imbue the characters with the Lotus Sutra's spirit of peace.

Saito: It seems that when we pursue the roots of Eastern civilization, ultimately we arrive at the Lotus Sutra.

Ikeda: Indeed. And even within so great a work of religious literature as the Lotus Sutra, the parable of the three kinds of medicinal herbs and two kinds of trees holds a unique interest. Among the seven parables of the Lotus Sutra, it alone emphasizes the diversity of living beings. Through this emphasis, it highlights the equality of the Buddha's compassion.

The Buddha's compassion is perfectly equal and impartial. The Buddha views all beings as his own children and strives to elevate them to attain his same enlightened state of life.

It's not that there are no differences among people. Rather, it's that the Buddha, while fully recognizing people's differences, does not discriminate among them. The Buddha respects people's individuality and desires that they may freely manifest their unique qualities. He is neither partial nor adverse toward people on account of their individual proclivities. The Buddha loves, rejoices at and tries to bring out each person's uniqueness; this is his compassion and his wisdom.

Suda: In "Medicinal Herbs," Shakyamuni explains:

> I look upon all things
> as being universally equal,
> I have no mind to favor this or that,
> to love one or hate another.
> I am without greed or attachment
> and without limitation or hindrance.
> At all times, for all things
> I preach the Law equally;
> as I would for a single person,
> that same way I do for numerous persons. (LS5, 103)

He states that the Buddha equally expounds the Law for all beings; and that he expounds the Law to many people without partiality, just as he would for an individual.

Ikeda: The important point is that the Buddha's preaching begins from a recognition of human diversity. The Buddha asks the question: How can I enable each person to attain Buddhahood, notwithstanding differences in circumstance, temperament and capacity? The Lotus Sutra, without departing in the least from the reality of the individual, clarifies the path to Buddhahood for all.

The humanism of the Lotus Sutra comes down to the tenet of treasuring the individual. This is the Buddha's spirit. The Lotus Sutra's fundamental objective of universal enlightenment begins with treasuring the individual and can be realized only through steadfast adherence to this point.

To love people or love humanity in the abstract is easy. To feel compassion toward real individuals is difficult.

The great Russian author Fyodor Dostoevsky points to this seeming contradiction in the sentiments expressed by a character in one of his novels: "The greater my love of mankind in general, the less I love people in particular, that is to say, separately, as individuals."[12] And elsewhere he says, "In abstract love for humanity one almost always loves no one but oneself."[13]

The Soka Gakkai, without ever departing from the individual human being, has been fighting to enable all people to realize absolute happiness. This is a lofty endeavor that will shine brilliantly in the annals of human history.

Endo: In a practical sense, the Lotus Sutra exists here and now within the Soka Gakkai.

Incidentally, why is it that people, whose lives are so precious, are allegorically represented as plants and trees? This point may be difficult to understand.

Ikeda: Yes. The same could be said of comparing the Buddha to a cloud. To fathom this particular allegory, consider the climate and culture of India.

Suda: The weather in India is divided into three seasons, dry, hot and rainy. The rainy season lasts for about four months, and there is very little rainfall during the remaining eight months of the year.

As a result, rain is eagerly awaited and comes, quite literally, as a blessing. Perhaps for that reason, we find many examples in the Buddhist scriptures—as with the "Dharma rain" here in the "Medicinal Herbs" chapter—where the Buddha's teaching is compared to rain.

Endo: In India, I understand, when it rains, people customarily say that the weather is good.

In 1992, I accompanied you, President Ikeda, on your trip to India. It rained on the day of our arrival. I was discouraged at this, but everyone else was delighted. I was told that in India there is a saying that rain falls when an honored guest is received. It was a minor incident of culture shock.

Saito: We Japanese tend to write off rain as unfortunate. But in light of the cultural and religious background of India, the comparison of the Buddha to a great cloud makes perfect sense. Since before the advent of Buddhism, the Vedic god Indira,[14] who is said to cause rainfall and is also associated with lightning, has commanded the Indian people's greatest affection and reverence. It's conceivable that the comparison of the Buddha to a cloud draws upon this image. Thus, in "Medicinal Herbs," we find the passage:

> This beneficent cloud is laden with moisture,
> the lightning gleams and flashes,
> and the sound of thunder reverberates afar,
> causing the multitude to rejoice. (LS5, 101)

Ikeda: The "sound of thunder" is the Buddha's great, compassionate voice with which he seeks to lead people to happiness. A cloud that covers the sky and sends rain down is indeed an apt metaphor for the Buddha who lovingly protects all people.

In any event, this discussion underlines just how important it is to be sensitive to the many differences—cultural, historical and geographical—in people's experiences. For instance, there are places where even an analogy so seemingly straightforward as "faith that is like fire versus faith like water" will not make sense to all people. People of other countries won't necessarily understand or agree with something simply on the rationale that "this is how it's done in Japan."

We need to rack our brains to figure out how Buddhism can be made understandable to people of different cultures and backgrounds. This is the spirit of Buddhism; it is the exact opposite of self-complacence.

As for the comparison of living beings with plants and trees, since in India there are long periods during which no rain falls, raising plants and trees requires considerable effort. And, in like measure, plants and trees are highly prized. People—precious beings all—are likened to plants and trees because they are similarly guided toward Buddhahood by the strenuous efforts of the Buddha.

Endo: In his *Treatise on the Great Perfection of Wisdom*, the great Indian Buddhist scholar Nagarjuna uses the image of "severing [the roots of] plants or trees" to describe the spirit of not begrudging one's life [in making offerings to the Law]. Even in this expression, we sense a reverence for plants and trees as things possessing life and as important in some sense on a par with human beings.

Suda: This brings us to the question of why this chapter is titled "The Parable of the Medicinal Herbs." Medicinal herbs certainly figure prominently in the parable of the three kinds of medicinal herbs and two kinds of trees; but in the text of the chapter, the term *medicinal herbs* is mentioned along with plants, bushes, thickets, groves and trees large and small (cf. LS5, 101). Wouldn't "Parable of the Trees" or "Parable of the Plants and Trees" make an equally suitable title?

Ikeda: So it would seem. As a matter of fact, the part of the Lotus Sutra in Sanskrit corresponding to the "Medicinal Herbs" chapter contains a section that does not appear in Kumarajiva's translation, though it is included in other Chinese translations.

Saito: It's a fairly lengthy passage. And in it there is heightened focus on medicinal herbs.

Ikeda: It says in one place, "In the Snow Mountains, the king of mountains, there are four kinds of medicinal herbs."[15]

The Snow Mountains are the Himalayas. The great Snow Mountains certainly have a regal appearance. They have a dignity like that of someone who has realized total victory. It seems most appropriate that this land should have been the birthplace of Shakyamuni, who attained the supreme summit of human existence.

In the Sanskrit text, "Medicinal Herbs" tells the story of how a physician goes into the Himalayas in search of herbs to cure a man who has been blind since birth.

Saito: The four kinds of medicinal herbs said to be found in the Himalayas are called (1) "Storing the Causes of All Color and Flavor," (2) "Curing All Ills," (3) "Removing All Poisons" and (4) "Giving Peace and Comfort From the Symptoms of Every Disease."

Thanks to the medicinal herbs, the man regains his sight and is delighted. He succumbs, however, to the illusion that, because he can see, he has complete understanding of all things in the world.

Ikeda: The man's blindness signifies the state of life of those immersed in the sufferings of the six paths.[16] His condition after the blindness is cured signifies the state of life of those who have freed themselves from the endless cycle of transmigration in the six paths of existence. Such beings include those who are satisfied with the enlightenment of the world of Learning and those who are comfortable dwelling in the state of Realization. The point, however, is that all people should aspire to supreme enlightenment, that is, the state of Buddhahood.

Suda: The physician in the story, then, represents the Buddha.

Ikeda: Yes. In "Life Span" as well, the Buddha is described as a "skilled physician." The Buddha is a great physician of existence and of human life.

The Chinese character for *medicine* has two parts. The top part means "herb" and the bottom "comfort." Medicine cures life's ills and gives comfort. This is a simple analysis of the characters and is not a strict etymology.

Endo: The important thing is what precisely is the "medicine" that can impart supreme and indestructible peace and ease?

Ikeda: That's right. Nichiren Daishonin says, "'Medicine' means the 'medicine of excellent color and fragrance of Nam-myoho-renge-kyo'" (GZ, 824).

He also says, "Without doubt the great beneficial medicine of the Mystic Law will cure the great disease of ignorance that afflicts all people" (GZ, 720). Nam-myoho-renge-kyo is the "secret medicine" for fundamentally leading all people to enlightenment. This is the essential point of "Medicinal Herbs."

THE BUDDHA EMBRACES ALL BEINGS WITH HIS COMPASSIONATE WISDOM

Saito: The Buddha, while understanding the differences among living beings, expounds the one Buddha vehicle that benefits all equally. The "Medicinal Herbs" chapter calls the Buddha, who possesses such wisdom, "one who knows all things" (LS5, 98) and emphasizes the Buddha's wisdom, which is a "wisdom that embraces all species" (LS5, 100).

Ikeda: Since the Buddha is "one who knows all things," he can expound all manner of teachings and correctly guide all people. Moreover, he raises people in such a way as to enable them to acquire the same universal knowledge that he possesses; that is, to attain the state of Buddhahood.

Endo: Such knowledge sounds a lot like the faculty of omniscience that Christians attribute to God. What is the difference between these two kinds of knowing?

Ikeda: As you point out, in Christianity the perfect wisdom of the Creator is termed "omniscience." The argument seems to go that since all things were created by this divine being, he is all-knowing.

The Buddha's encompassing knowledge is not of this kind. There are various interpretations, but I believe that the Buddha's knowledge of all things refers to his wisdom to completely and thoroughly understand all living beings and what teachings should be expounded to them; and that he possesses this wisdom because of his compassion to lead all people to happiness. The Buddha's knowledge of all things could be called "wisdom that is one with compassion."

On this point, I find the interpretation given in the Buddhist text the *Milindapanha* (The Questions of King Menander) most enlightening. It explains that the Buddha can know all things because he concentrates so intently on what he wishes to know. It is not the case that he knows everything from the outset.

Since the Buddha knows the true entity of his own life, when he directs his heart toward an individual, he understands the person's thoughts and sufferings as well as everything necessary to lead him or her to enlightenment—including the teaching through which the person can advance toward Buddhahood.

Because of his compassion, the Buddha directs his heart toward the people. His spirit is to lead all suffering beings to happiness without fail. In this spirit of affection and concern for others, the Buddha is like a parent desperately trying to protect his children. From such compassion, boundless wisdom arises. I think this is the nature of the Buddha's all-encompassing wisdom.

Saito: I fully agree. In a pre-Lotus Sutra scripture called the Sutta-nipata, Shakyamuni, discussing how those who have mastered the way of living in accord with the highest ideal ought to conduct themselves, says: "May all beings be happy and secure, may their hearts be wholesome!... Just as a mother would protect her only child at the risk of her own life, even so, let him cultivate a boundless heart towards all beings.... Let his thoughts of boundless love pervade the whole world...."[17]

Ikeda: Those who have attained true enlightenment do not close themselves off in that enlightenment but manifest a spirit of infinite compassion. They yearn for the happiness of all people and the peace and tranquility of the entire world. If this is not the case, then it is not true enlightenment. Therefore, Shakyamuni left behind words such as these as a guide for practitioners to ensure that they would not get stuck in a shallow enlightenment or confuse a false sense of enlightenment for the real thing.

The Buddha's enlightenment and wisdom are inseparable from his infinite compassion. Isn't this principle of "compassion manifesting as wisdom" and "wisdom manifesting as compassion" what the Lotus Sutra means by "wisdom embracing all species"?

Endo: Then we can take the passage in "Medicinal Herbs," "I am one who knows all things, sees all things, understands the way, opens the way, preaches the way" (LS5, 98), as pointing to this oneness of wisdom and compassion. It indicates that the Buddha who "knows all things" simultaneously understands the way, opens the way and preaches the way.

Ikeda: A Buddhist leader has to "understand," "open" and "preach" the way. A true leader uses all three categories of action—physical (opening the way), verbal (preaching the way) and mental (understanding the way)—to develop and expand the widespread propagation of the Mystic Law.

Suda: T'ien-t'ai interprets "one who knows all things" as indicating one who possesses in his or her heart the three kinds of wisdom: the wisdom to understand the universal aspect of all phenomena, the wisdom to understand the individual aspects of all phenomena, and the wisdom to understand both as well as the truth that permeates them.

Of these, the wisdom to understand the universal aspect of all phenomena is the wisdom to perceive the truth of nonsubstantiality. It indicates the wisdom to understand that, in essence, all things are nonsubstantial and impermanent without discrimination. This is the wisdom of voice-hearers and *pratyekabuddhas*, and it is also called the wisdom of nonsubstantiality.

The wisdom to understand the individual aspects of all phenomena is the wisdom to perceive the truth of temporary existence. This is the wisdom of bodhisattvas who, based on the realization that all things are essentially nonsubstantial, understand the diversity of individual entities that temporarily come into existence. Bodhisattvas require this wisdom because they have to lead people to happiness amid the realities of life.

The wisdom to understand both the universal and individual aspects of all phenomena is the wisdom of the Buddha, who possesses both and can employ them at will and without error. This is the wisdom of the Middle Way.

T'ien-t'ai calls the perfect possession of these three kinds of wisdom "three kinds of wisdom in a single mind" and says that this state can be achieved through Buddhist practice. T'ien-t'ai's interpretation again underlines the point that the Buddha's wisdom is at one with his compassion to lead all people to happiness.

Ikeda: No matter how people may insist they have attained enlightenment, if they do not behave compassionately, then they are lying. Wisdom is invisible. A person's conduct, therefore, is the yardstick or barometer for gauging his or her wisdom. The purpose of the Buddha's appearance in the world, after all, is accomplished through his behavior as a human being.

Suda: When we look at the appallingly uncompassionate conduct of people such as Nikken,[18] it becomes only too plain that they are entirely lacking in wisdom.

Ikeda: The wisdom to understand the universal as well as the individual aspects of all phenomena—that is to say, "wisdom manifesting as compassion"—is the wisdom of the Buddha who has attained thorough mastery of his own life.

In Kiyoshi Miki's *Jinseiron Noto* (Thoughts on Life), a book I read avidly in my youth, there is the line, "Understanding yourself eventually leads to understanding others."[19] To the extent that we contemplate ourselves and elevate our state of life, we can deepen our understanding of others.

Someone with a high state of life is capable of recognizing and treasuring people's individuality. A person of wisdom tries to invigorate and bring out the best in others.

Those who appear to have wisdom but who lack compassion cannot invigorate others. On the contrary, they develop a cruel and cunning "wisdom" and do others harm. Theirs is not genuine wisdom.

Life embodies the mutual possession of the Ten Worlds and of the principle that a single moment of life possesses three thousand realms; that is, the entire universe.

A Buddha, who perceives the true entity of his own life, naturally manifests the spirit to treasure the lives of all beings as highly as his own or as he would his own children. The spirit to make the entire world, the entire universe, peaceful and tranquil wells forth in his life. This is the Buddha's compassion; and the Buddha's compassion is inseparable from his wisdom.

In "Medicinal Herbs," Shakyamuni expresses this spirit as follows: "Those who have not yet crossed over [to the shore of enlightenment] I will cause to cross over, those not yet freed [from illusion] I will free, those not yet at rest I will put at rest" (LS5, 98).

And in another passage:

I appear in the world
like a great cloud
that showers moisture upon
all the dry and withered living beings,
so that all are able to escape suffering,
gain the joy of peace and security,
the joys of this world
and the joy of nirvana. (LS5, 102)

I think it could be said that the essence of the one Buddha vehicle is the Buddha's great life-condition of wisdom at one with compassion. In "Medicinal Herbs," this essence is represented as a great cloud and as rain that falls equally upon all.

Regarding the rain that equally moistens all the various plants and trees, the chapter says that the Buddha "[causes] the Dharma rain to rain on all equally" (LS5, 103). Nichiren Daishonin indicates that this passage can be interpreted in two ways. When emphasis is placed on the Buddha, it refers to the "equal compassion of Shakyamuni Buddha." But when the Dharma rain is emphasized, it indicates the "equal and great wisdom of Myoho-renge-kyo" (GZ, 828).

TOWARD A CENTURY OF "HUMAN FLOWERS" IN FULL BLOOM

Saito: It is the Buddha's immense life-state of wisdom at one with compassion that equally "moistens" the lives of all people in their infinite diversity.

Ikeda: Yes. They are moistened, or nourished, by the compassion of the mentor, the Buddha. And they themselves develop as entities of compassion. Human beings nourish human beings. Life nourishes life.

At the close of "Medicinal Herbs," it says:

The Law preached by the Buddha
is comparable to a great cloud
which, with a single-flavored rain,
moistens human flowers
so that each is able to bear fruit. (LS5, 105)

I like the expression "human flowers." It conveys an image of the blossoming of a multitude of people, each possessing rich individuality.

Shakyamuni doubtless perceived the unique character of each person as distinctly as the unique fruit and shades of flowers produced by trees as diverse as cherry, plum, peach and damson. I hope that by studying the "Medicinal Herbs" chapter we can learn about the Buddha's spirit to recognize and treasure the uniqueness in each individual.

This directly relates to the matter of creating harmony amid diversity, a fundamental issue of the twenty-first century. While highly respecting the unique characteristics of different races and cultures, we have to create solidarity based on our common humanity. In the absence of such solidarity, the human race has no future. Diversity should beget not conflict in the world but richness. And the humanism of the Lotus Sutra, which finds concrete expression in a merciful temperament, holds the key.

In the movement for Indian independence, how did Mahatma Gandhi move so many people to action? I believe that the fundamental cause lay in his character, which was polished by his wholehearted dedication to and tenacious struggles for truth. Gandhi's character "moistened" the hearts of the people. An episode well illustrates this.

Once when an important political conference was about to begin, Gandhi was found nervously searching around for something. When someone asked him what he was looking for, Gandhi replied, "I've lost my pencil." Since there was no time, the person offered him another pencil to use. But Gandhi, saying, "I cannot lose that pencil," continued searching. The pencil, which was at length discovered, turned out to be an old pencil only about three centimeters long. It had been donated to Gandhi's movement by a small child.[20]

For Gandhi, the tiny pencil was not a pencil at all. It was a beautiful heart. Therefore, he could not simply throw it away. It seems to me that Gandhi's "secret," the reason why this man, whom people revered as the Mahatma (Great Soul), was at the same time affectionately known by the familiar nickname "Bapu" (Father) lay in his remarkable sincerity.

I would not treat lightly even a single piece of paper that is imbued with the members' sincerity. In response to a sincere offering of white rice that he received, Nichiren Daishonin writes, "You should realize from this that polished rice is not polished rice, it is life itself" (WND, 1126).

In a truly humane world, even inanimate things are not merely objects. They are life, a reflection of our hearts. And human beings themselves are the most precious of all.

Saito: It seems that Gandhi's trust in the people knew no bounds. With the conviction that what is possible for one person is possible for all, he espoused the ideal of nonviolence and organized a large-scale popular movement.

Ikeda: A movement or organization will not long survive if it is held together only by decrees or rules. And it will fare still worse if the attempt is made to move people by force.

Only if we respect one another's individuality, share one another's joys and sorrows, and mutually inspire one another with courage and hope can we unite in solidarity. It is such a spirit of harmony and sense of inspiration that makes a true popular movement possible.

Endo: The term *organization* conjures up images of conformity. But in this day and age, not many people will be attracted to a body or group that demands rigid conformity.

Ikeda: Exactly. A popular movement has to be guided on the most fundamental level by humanism.

Suda: A fresh, vibrant humanism has been at the heart of the Soka Gakkai's development. This is the honest feeling shared by those of my generation who have grown up from childhood practicing with the organization.

Ikeda: I suppose that this is a natural outcome. Toward that end, I am struggling with all my might every hour and every moment of each day to cause the organization to pulse with the Buddhist spirit of compassion. It is imperative that SGI leaders never neglect this painstaking work, never lose this sense of responsibility.

Suda: The essence of the organization exists nowhere apart from the human being, which is its nucleus.

When we read the Gosho, we see that the Daishonin gives guidance to a wide spectrum of disciples and followers based on a truly meticulous grasp of their unique character and personality. Thanks to the Gosho, we know, for example, of Shijo Kingo's short temper.

Ikeda: This shows just how concerned the Daishonin was about each of his followers.

To Shijo Kingo, he shows very detailed concern, sounding almost like a parent instructing a child. The Daishonin advises him, for instance, to avoid drinking when away from home (WND, 461) and warns him not to quarrel with the women in his household, even if they happen to be at fault (GZ, 1176).

And when the elder of the Ikegami brothers, Munenaka, was disowned by his father for the second time, the Daishonin, while deeply concerned about the ability of the younger Ikegami, Munenaga, to maintain his faith, writes to the latter in a way that, at a glance, sounds like a stern rejection: "This time I am sure that you will give up your faith. If you do, I have not the slightest intention of reproaching you for it. Likewise, neither should you blame me, Nichiren, when you have fallen into hell" (WND, 636).

Without really understanding and grasping another's heart, one could not hope to communicate his or her true intent by making such a declaration. The Daishonin not only completely grasped the conflict raging in the heart of Munenaga, who stood at a great crossroads in his life, but he also doubtless had a minute understanding of his personality.

Endo: In particular, I am always profoundly impressed by how deeply the Daishonin understood the sentiments of parents who had lost children, even though he never married or had children of his own. Some of his letters of encouragement to bereaved families come to mind.

Ikeda: The Daishonin is truly a great Buddha. He understands in its totality the reality of each person's life and deeply shares their sufferings. He absolutely never gives abstract guidance as though foisting set answers on people.

As a result, there are instances where it may appear that he is telling one person the exact opposite of what he is saying to someone else.

He urges the wife of Toki Jonin, who was suffering from illness but was not inclined to consult a physician, to seek medical treatment, explaining the importance of living a long life: "If he died young, even a man whose wisdom shone as brilliantly as the sun would be less than a living dog" (WND, 955). But to the spirited Shijo Kingo, a Kamakura samurai who was ready to die for his honor, the Daishonin emphasizes that gaining honor as a Buddhist and as a member of society is more important than longevity.

Suda: He says, "It is better to live a single day with honor than to live to 120 and die in disgrace" (WND, 851).

Ikeda: In either case, it is guidance of compassion at one with wisdom arising from the Daishonin's spirit of compassion for his disciples. Both statements are true. This is the spirit of "Medicinal Herbs."

Behind his guidance to Shijo Kingo, Nichiren Daishonin, in his heart, probably wanted to tell his disciple to conduct himself wisely each day, aware of his tendency to be short-tempered. Had Shijo Kingo failed to do so, his very life could have been in danger.

It is not only his actions as the votary of the Lotus Sutra who underwent great persecutions that match the spirit outlined in the Lotus Sutra. When we read the Gosho with careful attention to detail, we can see how the humanism of the Lotus Sutra also comes to life in the Daishonin's conduct.

The Daishonin lashed out with burning indignation and strictly admonished the authorities and the religious figures in league with them, who were causing the people suffering. This has long been used as grounds for labeling the Daishonin's Buddhism as "intolerant" or "exclusive." But this perspective is utterly one-sided.

Both the Daishonin's merciful guidance to his followers and his strict remonstrations with the authorities are pervaded with a living humanism.

Saito: In your speeches over the past ten years or so, President Ikeda, while you have cited a great many Gosho, it seems to me that you have consistently focused on the Daishonin's humanism.

Ikeda: I quote and discuss the Gosho out of my desire to convey to the entire world the supreme humanity, the vast and immense state of life of the Daishonin, who declared, "The various sufferings of all humankind are the sufferings of the one person Nichiren" (GZ, 758).

In "The Parable of the Medicinal Herbs," it says that the great cloud of the Buddha's compassion "covers" the entire thousand-millionfold world, that is, the entire universe. How can we cause the immense love and compassion of the original Buddha to rain down upon the entire world? This is the thought that constantly occupies my mind; this is my constant determination. Carrying out the work of the Buddha is the SGI's mission. Our struggle now begins in earnest; we are now at last entering the essential phase of the movement for kosen-rufu.

I think that to revitalize the world, which today seems to be deadlocked, people have to think in terms of a universal perspective, recognizing the essential oneness of their lives with the universe. When they do, they will also perceive a oneness with nature and with the planet. Views of society, nationality and race will also naturally be revised in light of such a perspective on human life.

As long as the window of the human heart remains battened closed, no great future lies in store. People have to throw open the window. When they do so, there will be no further hindrance to peace.

The lives of all people are one with the universe. All the workings of the universe contribute to the individuality of each person. To put it another way, each person is a microcosm that reflects the macrocosm uniquely; fundamentally, the individual encompasses all. Therefore, each person is precious and irreplaceable.

The ultimate wisdom to understand this secret of life is the Buddha's wisdom to understand both the universal and individual aspects of all phenomena, the Buddha's great and impartial wisdom. The Buddha perceives that each person, each living entity, is equally precious.

I am confident that this humanism of the Lotus Sutra is the universal humanism that will hold the key for the next millennium.

The great Indian poet Rabindranath Tagore writes:

> *The same stream of life that runs through my veins night and day runs through the world and dances in rhythmic measures. It is the same life that shoots in joy through the dust of the earth in numberless blades of grass and breaks into tumultuous waves of leaves and flowers.*

It is the same life that is rocked in the ocean-cradle of birth and of death, in ebb and in flow.
I feel my limbs are made glorious by the touch of this world of life. And my pride is from the life-throb of ages dancing in my blood this moment.[21]

Let us continue joyfully and exuberantly advancing with the fundamental rhythm of the universe pulsing in our lives.

NOTES

1. Elise Boulding, *The Future; Images and Processes* (Thousand Oaks, CA: Sage Publications, Inc., 1995), p. 144.

2. Ibid., p. 146.

3. Ibid.

4. Ibid., p. 154.

5. Also known as Mahakashyapa.

6. Subhuti, Katyayana (or Mahakatyayana) and Maudgalyayana.

7. This parable concerns the replacement of the three vehicles of Learning, Realization and Bodhisattva with the one vehicle of Buddhahood.

8. Presentation and mastery: In the "Record of the Orally Transmitted Teachings," the Daishonin states: "The word *presentation* pertains to Kashyapa, to whom the teachings were presented. The word *master* [or completion] pertains to Shakyamuni, who acknowledges Kashyapa's mastery of them. Thus 'presentation and mastery' signifies that Kashyapa and Shakyamuni Buddha have attained an identical level of understanding" (GZ, 729).

9. Purna: One of Shakyauni's ten major disciples who was known as the foremost in preaching the Law. Purna belongs to the last of the three groups of voice-hearers who understood the Buddha's teaching by

hearing "The Parable of the Phantom City" chapter about their past relationship with Shakyamuni major world system dust particle *kalpas* earlier.

10. Jin Yong: Pen name of Louis Cha (1924–).

11. A monument to a nuclear-free world planned for at the Soka Gakkai's Chugoku Memorial Park in Hiroshima.

12. Fyodor Dostoevsky (1821–81), *The Karamazov Brothers* (Moscow: Raduga Publishers, 1990), p. 76.

13. Dostoevsky, *The Idiot*, trans. Constance Garnett (London: William Heineman, 1913), p. 457.

14. Indira, chief of the Vedic gods of of India, was originally the god of thunder and one of the central deities in ancient Indian mythology.

15. Zuiryu Nakamura, *Gendaigo Yaku Hokekyo Jo* (The Lotus Sutra in Modern Translation, Part 1) (Tokyo: Shunjusha, 1995), p. 131.

16. Six paths: The six lower worlds of Hell, Hunger, Animality, Anger, Humanity and Heaven.

17. The Sutta-nipata, trans. H. Saddhatissa (London: Curzon Press, 1985), pp. 15–16.

18. Nikken: Current high priest of Nichiren Shoshu.

19. Kiyoshi Miki, *Jinseiron Noto* (Tokyo: Shinchosha, 1954), p. 147.

20. Tatsuo Morimoto, *Ganji to Tagoru* (Gandhi and Tagore) (Tokyo: Daisan Bunmeisha, 1995), p. 67.

21. Rabindranath Tagore, *Gitanjali: Song Offerings* (Delhi: Macmillan Indian Limited, 1985), pp. 46–47.

PART FOUR

"Bestowal of Prophecy" Chapter

4 The Purpose of "Bestowal of Prophecy" Is To Enable All People To Enter the Path of Absolute Happiness

Saito: I would like to do my best to make our current dialogue on the Lotus Sutra something that members throughout the world can use at discussion meetings and in conducting Buddhist dialogue.

Ikeda: I completely agree. Let's redouble our efforts.

The discussion meeting is like a great river, and all activities are like tributaries that flow into this river. Activities to broaden the circle of friends in society and meetings of various kinds for faith and study all contribute to the great river of the discussion meeting. This broad and deep river, created by the confluence of these myriad streams, flows into the ocean of the century of the people. On its banks, vast fertile plains of human culture will produce rich fruit of many kinds.

The heart of the SGI is found in the discussion meeting. President Toda said: "The first president [Tsunesaburo Makiguchi] would be the first to arrive at the meeting place. When someone else arrived, he would engage the person in discussion. When a second person came, he would speak with the two of them, and when a third came, he would talk with those three, instructing them in all matters with the greatest kindness and courtesy."[1] He also once said: "It's fine even if there's just one person [at a meeting]. The important thing is that we earnestly and energetically explain the teaching, relate our experience to that one person, and wholeheartedly discuss kosen-rufu and life. Even if there are just two people, if they each go home from the meeting with a sense of joy and fulfillment from having discussed the Gohonzon and inspired one another, then it's a success. If three people come to a meeting, you should consider it well attended."[2]

Suda: While good attendance is important, the crucial point is to create discussion meetings where each person feels truly satisfied and leaves with the desire to come to another meeting, perhaps bringing a friend next time.

Ikeda: We shouldn't badger people to attend the meeting simply to get a good turnout; the thing is to connect with one another on the level of the heart. Discussion means one-to-one dialogue. It is essential, therefore, that each person be treasured. This is the key to generating a rhythm of lively, successful discussion meetings.

We don't speak of the "tradition" of the discussion meeting simply because the pattern of holding such meetings has continued for many years. Rather, with the discussion meeting as the central focus of our activities, we have striven to treasure each person; this spirit to value and respect the individual is the tradition of the SGI. The SGI has unceasingly encouraged people in their ordinary yet valiant struggles. This is the tradition of the discussion meeting.

From a societal viewpoint, the number of people participating in these meetings is not large; nor is any particular attention paid to these meetings. Indeed, no gathering of people is more simple or down-to-earth. But discussion meetings are grounded in a philosophy that thoroughly explains the Law pervading the universe. They produce a nourishing moisture that nurtures the lives of people from all walks of life, enabling them to blossom. They are pervaded with hope that inspires people — no matter how overwhelmed they may be — with the spirit to stand up and try again.

Endo: They leave one feeling wonderfully refreshed and exhilarated.

Ikeda: That is the ideal.

A young man may rush to get to a meeting after working hard all day. The moment he arrives, he may relax, thinking, "I made it in time," and suddenly become drowsy. But his drowsiness won't last long because a perennially kind but firm women's division district leader is sure to tell him: "Show a little life! You're still young, after all."

There are pioneer members who explain the great joy of faith with poignant words infused with rich experience. And there are children in the Boys and Girls Group who are delightful, even if sometimes they may make a commotion.

There may be a father who comes to a meeting for the first time in ages, attributing his presence to the constant needling of his spouse. And when, beaming, he announces his determination to "finally get serious about my practice," his wife, amid the applause, smiles tearfully.

There is laughter, there are tears, there is emotion. The SGI discussion meeting is a people's oasis that reverberates with a spirit of determination and appreciation, where suffering turns into courage, and fatigue gives way to warm fulfillment.

This small gathering is the very image of human harmony. It is a true model of democracy. It has the pulse of kosen-rufu and links faith, family and the community. It is pervaded with the spirit to enable the noble children of the Buddha and their precious friends to become happy. This is the spirit of the Lotus Sutra.

Endo: As you have described in *The New Human Revolution*, your efforts for world kosen-rufu, President Ikeda, began with your attending a discussion meeting in the United States.

Suda: As you write in *The New Human Revolution*, too, it seems to me that Shakyamuni's first expounding of the Law for a small group of former fellow ascetics was also a kind of discussion meeting. There were five participants in addition to Shakyamuni. This very small gathering marked the brilliant dawn of Buddhism. Also, it is said that to get to the place where his former companions were pursuing their ascetic practice, Shakyamuni walked more than a hundred miles.

Ikeda: The Buddha's preaching took the format of dialogue. In this we find an important point in common with SGI discussion meetings.

And the Lotus Sutra itself, the summation of Shakyamuni's preaching, could be thought of as a grand discussion meeting. To people searching for and earnestly inquiring into the meaning of life, Shakyamuni replies with sincerity, relating his own experience and skillfully employing metaphors and parables to clarify his meaning. Those who see and hear this give-and-take are engulfed in the joy of expanding their own states of life. There is a radiant determination, a spiritual chain reaction, a wondrous heart-to-heart exchange.

How does Shakyamuni cause the eternal sun of the Mystic Law to rise in people's hearts at this "discussion meeting"? An important focus in answering this is the concept of "bestowal of prophecy." Today, therefore, let us discuss "Bestowal of Prophecy," the sixth chapter.

The Bestowal of Prophecy Upon the Four Great Voice-hearers

> If, because you understand our innermost minds,
> you bestow a prophecy of Buddhahood upon us,
> it would be like sweet dew bathing us,
> washing away fever and imparting coolness.
> Suppose that someone coming from a land of famine
> should suddenly encounter a great king's feast.
> His heart still filled with doubt and fear,

he would not dare to eat the food at once,
but if he were instructed by the king to do so,
then he would venture to eat. (LS6, 110)

Endo: "Bestowal of prophecy" refers to Shakyamuni's conferring upon his disciples words of assurance that in the future they are certain to attain Buddhahood.

In "Bestowal of Prophecy," Shakyamuni confers prophecies of enlightenment upon the four great voice-hearer disciples— Kashyapa,[3] Subhuti, Katyayana[4] and Maudgalyayana. This is the second bestowal of prophecy in the sutra, the first having been the prophecy of enlightenment for Shariputra in "Simile and Parable," the third chapter. Also, this in a sense brings to a conclusion Shakyamuni's preaching to the four great voice-hearers, which begins in "Simile and Parable" when he expounds the parable of the three carts and the burning house.[5]

ACCEPTING AND UPHOLDING THE LAW IS ITSELF ENLIGHTENMENT

Saito: Members often ask what, specifically, attaining Buddhahood means. In Shakyamuni's predictions of enlightenment for the voice-hearers in the Lotus Sutra, the attainment of Buddhahood is presented as something that will happen in the distant future. By contrast, Nichiren Daishonin teaches that we can attain Buddhahood in this lifetime. In that case, what kind of state are we talking about?

Ikeda: That is a difficult question to answer, but to put it simply, attaining Buddhahood is not so much a matter of arriving at a destination or reaching a goal as internalizing the process of continually strengthening the world of Buddhahood in our lives. This is termed "entering the unsurpassed way."

In the theoretical teaching, or first half, of the Lotus Sutra, Shakyamuni had not yet departed from the view that attaining

Buddhahood necessitates practicing for countless aeons. So, naturally, the prophecies he makes for his disciples are of attaining enlightenment in the distant future. But Shakyamuni's true intention is to enable all people to advance along the same path as he. The bestowal of prophecy assures the Buddha's disciples that they have definitely entered the path of life, the road leading to absolute happiness, along which the Buddha himself has traveled.

This is not the enlightenment expounded in the earlier sutras or the theoretical teaching (first half) of the Lotus Sutra; it is not a matter of becoming a Buddha "endowed with august attributes." Advancing along the same path as the Buddha is itself attaining Buddhahood.

Specifically, following the same path as the Buddha means accepting and upholding the Lotus Sutra; that is, to engrave in one's life the Buddha's spirit as revealed in the Lotus Sutra and to live in accord with that spirit. It means living in such a way as to never depart from the Buddha's spirit, under any and all circumstances. Such unwavering commitment ensures that we will never deviate from the Buddha way.

In "Supernatural Powers of the Thus Come One," Shakyamuni says:

> Therefore a person of wisdom,...
> after I have passed into extinction
> should accept and uphold this sutra.
> Such a person assuredly and without doubt
> will attain the Buddha way. (LS21, 276)

This means that those who accept and uphold the Lotus Sutra can advance without fail along the path of the Buddha and are certain to attain Buddhahood.

Saito: In a sense, the very question "What is the state of Buddhahood like?" reflects an understanding of enlightenment that is basically informed by the earlier sutras and the theoretical teaching of the Lotus Sutra. Often people suppose that Buddha-hood is a state of attainment, and that in attaining Buddhahood one becomes a radically different person. We may tend to think in these terms because we speak of someone becoming a Buddha.

Ikeda: That's right. Nichiren Daishonin teaches that Buddhahood is not a matter of *becoming* a Buddha but of revealing the Buddha in one's own life, of cultivating the life of Buddhahood within.

President Toda said: "Attaining Buddhahood does not mean becoming or trying to become a Buddha. It means honestly believing in the Daishonin's words that the common mortal is the supreme being and that all phenomena manifest the true entity and awakening to one's identity as a Buddha existing from the remote past and throughout the infinite future."

In "Bestowal of Prophecy," when Shakyamuni predicts enlightenment for Maudgalyayana, he speaks of a time "when he has cast off his present body" (LS6, 115). He says in effect that in future existences when Maudgalyayana has "shed his present body," he will practice under a great multitude of Buddhas and finally become a Buddha himself.

The Daishonin says regarding this passage: "To assert that one must cast off his or her present body before attaining Buddhahood is a doctrine of the provisional teachings. But the true act of 'casting off one's body' consists of casting aside feelings of attachment to such doctrines" (GZ, 731).

Also, the Daishonin says that "cast off" should be interpreted as meaning "offer up," and that "cast off his present body" means "offering up the five elements[6] [that make up one's body] to the Dharma-realm" (GZ, 731). The Dharma-realm is the universe, the world, all living beings. The five elements indicate life. To "offer up the five elements to the Dharma-realm" means to carry out the actions of bodhisattvas who offer their lives to bring benefit to others. In other words, following the path of the bodhisattva is itself attaining Buddhahood.

The essential teaching, or second half, of the Lotus Sutra presents a new view of attaining enlightenment. This is found in the revelation in the "Life Span" chapter that the Buddha enlightened from the remote past has, since attaining Buddhahood, been continuously carrying out bodhisattva practice. In becoming a Buddha, Shakyamuni did not cease to be a bodhisattva. In concrete terms, the Buddha's actions and stance in society consist of bodhisattva practice. Even after attaining enlightenment, the Buddha continues to adhere to the path of bodhisattva practice. This, in other words, is the Buddha way.

Saito: At the very end of "Life Span," the Buddha's wish to "cause living beings to gain entry into the unsurpassed way and quickly acquire the body of a Buddha" (LS16, 232) is expressed. We can take the expression "cause living beings to gain entry into the unsurpassed way" as meaning to enable them to attain enlightenment or acquire the Buddha's enlightened properties.

Ikeda: From the standpoint of the essential teaching, attaining Buddhahood is not so much a goal or a special state but a path. We could probably even go so far as to say that the only difference in someone's condition before and after attaining Buddhahood has to do with whether this path is firmly established in the person's life.

"Firmly establishing this path" means solidifying in our lives a spirit of yearning for the happiness of oneself and others and continuously taking constructive action with that spirit.

Suda: It will be wonderful when this spirit of seeking the happiness of both oneself and others becomes an integral part of all lives.

Saito: Your point about "firmly establishing the path" perfectly agrees with the original meaning of the words *bestowal of prophecy*.

Endo: The Chinese character for *prophecy* is a verb originally meaning "to clearly distinguish and give coherent expression to." The term *bestowal of prophecy* appearing in the Chinese translation of the Lotus Sutra was coined by Kumarajiva when he rendered the sutra from the Indian language. In earlier translations, Chinese-character combinations meaning "expression of distinction" or "bestowal of decision" were used. Here, *distinction* means "clearly distinguishing"; and *decision* means "decisively judging."

Suda: "Bestowal of prophecy" is thought to originally derive from the Sanskrit word *vyakarana*, whose meanings include "distinction," "analysis" and "development." In Buddhist texts, it is used in the sense of giving a clear reply to a question.

Saito: In short, *prophecy*, in "bestowal of prophecy," means "clear statement." By stating things clearly, the Buddha enables people to advance unfailingly along the path to Buddhahood. In the chapter before last, we confirmed that belief and understanding indicate a spirit to advance and improve ourselves. By comparison, the "bestowal of prophecy" empowers us to engrave this spirit in the depths of our lives.

Ikeda: Originally, "bestowal of prophecy" meant giving a clear reply and so resolving the doubts in people's hearts. Leaders should always speak with forthrightness and clarity. Vagueness is bad, because it causes people to feel uneasy. Giving people confidence is the key point in the "bestowal of prophecy."

Saito: Most of the prophecies bestowed in Buddhist texts relate to conditions after death. Human beings cannot know with any certainty how things will be after death or in the future. This may have been precisely why it was necessary for Shakyamuni to speak clearly on these matters.

The Great Teacher T'ien-t'ai of China says that "bestowal of prophecy" refers to the Buddha's ability to "employ words and give people a true understanding."

Ikeda: The Buddha bestows prophecies upon people to cause them to clearly understand, to give them the awareness and confidence that they themselves can attain Buddhahood.

Suda: In the "Bestowal of Prophecy" chapter, Kashyapa is the first of the four great voice-hearers to receive a prediction of enlightenment. Observing the scene, Maudgalyayana and the others beseech Shakyamuni to bestow prophecies upon them as well. Shakyamuni then confers prophecies upon Subhuti, Katyayana and Maudgalyayana, in that order.

Endo: The parable of the great king's feast is related in the scene where Maudgalyayana and the other two voice-hearers request predictions of enlightenment.

With this parable, the three disciples explain that in asking the Buddha to bestow a prophecy of enlightenment upon them, they feel as though they were people from a land of famine who had suddenly encountered the feast of a great king, that is to say, the most exquisite and sumptuous cuisine. People in such a situation would be almost beside themselves with the desire to eat. But at the same time, so filled with doubt and fear would they be that they would dare not touch the food until the king has given them permission. In the same way, while these disciples have heard and accepted the teaching of the one Buddha vehicle that enables even voice-hearers to attain Buddhahood, they cannot feel true assurance unless the Buddha makes a clear prediction of enlightenment for them, too.

Suda: Incidentally, in this request spoken in unison by the three, Shakyamuni's giving a bestowal of prophecy is likened to "sweet dew." This is a translation of the Sanskrit term *amrita*, meaning "immortality," a mystic elixir of eternal youth and immortality said to exist in the realm of heaven. The use of this term implies that the bestowal of prophecy influences not only this life but future existences as well.

Ikeda: The bestowal of prophecy removes the unease the disciples had felt in the depths of their lives and gives them profound peace of mind. Through the bestowal of prophecy, which is the Buddha's assurance that they will ultimately attain Buddhahood, they gain profound confidence in the future.

It is probably to bolster this sense of confidence that the Buddha gives the title and the specific *kalpa* and land in which the four great voice-hearers will attain Buddhahood.

Saito: Shakyamuni indicates the name of the *kalpa* in which they will attain Buddhahood, the name of the land where they will attain Buddhahood, and the title they will assume as Buddhas. The prophecies bestowed upon the four great voice-hearers are as follows:

In a *kalpa* called Great Adornment and in a land called Light Virtue, Kashyapa will become a Buddha named Light Bright. In a *kalpa* called Possessed of Jewels and in a land called Jewel Born, Subhuti will become a Buddha named Rare Form. Katyayana will become a Buddha named Jambunada Gold[7] Light [no *kalpa* and land are given]. And in a *kalpa* called Joy Replete and in a land called Mind Delight, Maudgalyayana will become a Buddha named Tamalapatra[8] Sandalwood Fragrance.

While Shakyamuni says that he is bestowing prophecies on his disciples because of their dignity and virtue, it seems that the designations of the kalpa, land and name bear some relation to the particular strengths and personality of each of the disciples.

Ikeda: That's right. I think these designations encapsulate the drama of each one's life.

Suda: For example, in the case of Kashyapa, the first to receive a prophecy of the four, the word *light* (as in brilliance) is included in both his name, Light Bright, and in the name of the land, Light Virtue.

In Sanskrit, Light Bright has the sense of "shining glory." The name of the land, LightVirtue, means "world of honor" or "world replete with glory." And Great Adornment, the name of the kalpa, means "a figure of great brilliance."

Endo: Kashyapa was from a prestigious family, but he had in fact entered upon the life of a religious mendicant even earlier than Shakyamuni and had long led an itinerant life in search of truth. Eventually, he met Shakyamuni and is said to have decided to become his disciple the first time he saw him.

Tradition has it that because Shakyamuni wore clothes even coarser than his own, Kashyapa exchanged his own garments for Shakyamuni's, and that he then wore these exclusively. Kashyapa is said to have devoted himself to ascetic practices. And while it appears that some insensitive people among the Buddha's disciples looked down on Kashyapa because of his disheveled appearance, Shakyamuni behaved exactly the opposite. Respecting Kashyapa as someone who had practiced longer than he, Shakyamuni let him sit on an elevated seat identical to his own and praised him as the foremost in ascetic practice.

Ikeda: Shakyamuni, in other words, saw in Kashyapa, who had rigorously devoted himself to the most plain and arduous of practices, a person who shone most brightly.

Saito: Speaking of asceticism, in a parable found in the latter half of "The Parable of the Medicinal Herbs," in a section not contained in Kumarajiva's translation of the Lotus Sutra,[9] a man whose blindness has been cured by medicinal herbs from the Snow Mountains (Himalayas) is said to gain "the transcendental power to see for a thousand miles" by carrying out further ascetic practices.[10] In this parable, I think we can see a connection between ascetic practices and the name Light Bright.

Ikeda: The benefit of the blind man's ascetic practices is symbolic of the benefit that comes from believing in and understanding the Lotus Sutra. That benefit is to acquire a "light bright heart" that will remain ours eternally. This is the greatest treasure we can hope to possess.

The aim of the practice of asceticism is to dispel all desire concerning matters of clothing, food and shelter. The light of the Buddha's wisdom has the power to dispel the darkness of suffering in human life. It may be that Shakyamuni bestowed the name Light Bright Thus Come One on Kashyapa because this aspect of the Buddha's enlightenment coincides with the latter's strengths.

Nichiren Daishonin says: "Now, Nichiren and his followers illuminate the murk and darkness of slander of the Law with the light brightness of Nam-myoho-renge-kyo. This is in fact the virtue of Kashyapa, the Light Bright Thus Come One" (GZ, 731).

Propagating the Mystic Law that dispels the darkness of slander is itself the foremost ascetic practice.

Suda: In the prophecy bestowed on Subhuti, *jewel* becomes the key word. Jewel Born, the name of the land, literally means something that gives birth to or produces jewels. And the *kalpa* name, Possessed of Jewels, means "brilliance of jewels." Rare Form, Subhuti's title in that existence, means "one having the appearance worthy of renown."

Endo: Subhuti was the nephew of Sudatta, the wealthy merchant who built the famous Jetavana Monastery as an offering to Shakyamuni.[11] Subhuti is said to have become Shakyamuni's disciple upon meeting the Buddha when the monastery was first offered. Even after leaving secular life, Subhuti constantly offered whatever he could, and he was held to be the foremost in inner tranquillity and most worthy of receiving offerings.

Ikeda: Having excelled in the practice of almsgiving may connect Subhuti with the image of "jewels." But, more fundamentally, the recurrence of this word probably signifies the fact that, in the

Lotus Sutra, he gains the true "jewel of wisdom" and "jewel of life." In "Belief and Understanding," the fourth chapter, the four great voice-hearers delight at their discovery that the world of Buddhahood exists in their own lives, saying, "This cluster of unsurpassed jewels has come to us unsought" (LS4, 87).

Saito: It may be relevant that at the very start of "Belief and Understanding," Subhuti is called a man "of lifelong wisdom" (LS4, 80). Those of "lifelong wisdom" are those who base their lives on wisdom; it is another name for the Buddha. It also means "person of strong life force" and "person of longevity."

Subhuti excelled in wisdom. Among Shakyamuni's disciples, he was regarded as the foremost in understanding the doctrine of nonsubstantiality. Shakyamuni's preaching in many of the Wisdom sutras, which explain the doctrine of nonsubstantiality, is addressed to him. In particular, in the Great Wisdom Sutra and elsewhere, Shakyamuni goes so far as to direct Subhuti to instruct the bodhisattvas in the Buddha's perfect wisdom.

Ikeda: But Subhuti was himself still confined to the wisdom of the two vehicles. While he could explain the Buddha's wisdom to others, he did not seek to acquire the Buddha's perfect wisdom himself. In "Belief and Understanding," he reflects on his former attitude.

When he hears the Lotus Sutra, he can finally enter the path for gaining the Buddha's wisdom, that is, the path of Buddhahood. This is no doubt the reason why he receives the prophecy that he will become a renowned Buddha whose life shines with the inner "jewel" of the world of Buddhahood.

Suda: In the prophecy bestowed upon Katyayana, no mention is made of either the *kalpa* or the land; only his title, Jambunada Gold Light, is revealed. This name means "shining of gold dust from the Jambunada River." The Jambunada is a river through an idyllic realm said to lie on the northern side of the Snow

Mountains, called the Jambunada Forest. The gold dust taken from the river was supposed to shine with exceptional beauty.

Saito: It is related that Katyayana's skin shone with a beautiful golden hue. It seems to me he may have been given the name on this basis.

Ikeda: The name probably indicates the Buddha's character, which shines like gold with compassion and wisdom.

When we look at things in this way, we see that the disciples are given names that match their individual personalities. Their personal proclivities, moreover, are transformed into the virtuous qualities of the Buddhas they are destined to become.

Suda: Lastly, Maudgalyayana's name in the prophecy, Tamalapatra Sandalwood Fragrance, means "fragrance of the leaves of the tamala and sandalwood trees." The wood of these trees was pulverized and turned into perfume that was sprinkled on or applied to the body. The wood was also burned in festival fires.

The name of the *kalpa*, Joy Replete, means "abundant ease and joy." And Mind Delight, the name of the land, means "place that puts the mind at ease."

Endo: This *kalpa*, land and title would seem to relate to the fact that Maudgalyayana was known as the foremost in transcendental powers. There are many stories about his transcendental powers, but one episode in particular is often depicted in murals and other Buddhist art. That is when he causes King Brahma to revere and become a devotee of Shakyamuni.

As the story goes, Maudgalyayana once climbed up to the place in heaven where King Brahma and the other gods dwell and demonstrated to them meditation within a flame. The blinding light was so bright that not even King Brahma, who was held to personify the fundamental universal principle (Brahman), had ever seen anything like it. When Maudgalyayana declared himself to be a disciple of Shakyamuni, King Brahma asked through an intermediary whether there were many among Shakyamuni's disciples who possessed such great transcendental powers. Hearing that there were, King Brahma was overjoyed and vowed to become a follower of Shakyamuni. King Brahma, the ruler of the *saha* world, was greatly elated, and joy spread throughout and pervaded the entire world.

Ikeda: By showing his own power, the disciple of the Buddha taught King Brahma the greatness of his mentor, bringing honor to both mentor and disciple.

Suda: It may be because of the image of the flame in this episode that the title bestowed on Maudgalyayana incorporates the name of the wood burned in festival fires. Also, we can conjecture that the *kalpa* and age are named Joy Replete and Mind Delight, respectively, because the brilliance of this flame of Maudgalyayana's meditation filled the entire world with joy.

Ikeda: The important point here is that, upon attaining Buddhahood, the personality and total life experience of each of these disciples come to shine as virtuous enlightened attributes. As long as we have faith, no effort is wasted. This is the great benefit of the Lotus Sutra.

No doubt hearing the wonderful names of the *kalpa*, land and title—perfectly matching the character of each—enabled the four voice-hearers to sense profoundly that they would indeed attain Buddhahood. And all those around them could understand, by extension, that they, too, would become praiseworthy Buddhas. In consequence, ripples of joy spread among those who heard the bestowal of prophecies.

Suda: I am reminded of the SGI presentation of commendations to individuals for meritorious achievement. I am always moved by the heartfelt rejoicing of all participants at meetings where such awards are made and by how people, seeing their comrades and peers recognized in this way, determine to realize similar growth in their own lives.

Ikeda: Those selected to receive such recognition represent the entire membership. Therefore, a commendation awarded to one person is a commendation awarded to all who are advancing along the same path.

Even so, in these self-centered times, it is truly noble the way our members rejoice when their fellow members are honored, an event that becomes a source of inspiration for them to strive further in their own personal growth and development. Where else can you find such comradeship?

This is the world of the SGI, which is forged by strong faith. A spirit to applaud others arises from confidence in one's own life. By contrast, a spirit of envy reflects a lack of self-confidence.

Saito: Envy produces a kind of negative equality. Envious people try to hold others to their own low level, based on the model of "hammering down the nail that sticks out."

A spirit to applaud others produces true, positive equality. It manifests in the tendency to recognize all people, along with oneself, as noble and worthy of respect, and in the desire for all equally to grow. This, I believe, is the attitude of a genuine Buddhist.

Endo: This is what we find in the world of the Lotus Sutra. Shakyamuni teaches that all people can attain Buddhahood and urges them to advance together with him along the "unsurpassed way." Such a world emerges, it seems to me, because the Buddha revealed the one Buddha vehicle.

Ikeda: Precisely. The one Buddha vehicle is likened to an actual vehicle that takes us along the sure path toward the destination of

Buddhahood. It can stay on the correct path because it is propelled by the Buddha's compassion and guided by the Buddha's wisdom.

Entering the correct path leading to Buddhahood is the benefit of believing in and understanding the one Buddha vehicle of the Lotus Sutra. The bestowal of prophecy is the Buddha's assurance of this. These predictions of enlightenment, furthermore, elicit joy and confidence in others. In this way, the network of people advancing along the unsurpassed way of attaining Buddhahood expands further still. This is the world of the Lotus Sutra.

Endo: In fact, the number of those who receive prophecies of enlightenment steadily increases as the sutra progresses.

First, in "Simile and Parable," Shariputra alone receives such a prophecy. The four great voice-hearers see this and rejoice, and then they receive their own prophecies in the "Bestowal of Prophecy" chapter.

Next, in "Prophecy of Enlightenment for Five Hundred Disciples," the eighth chapter, similar predictions are bestowed on Purna and five hundred monks. In the following chapter, "Prophecies Conferred on Learners and Adepts," assurances of future enlightenment are conferred on Ananda, Rahula and two thousand disciples.

Thus, in the preaching from "Expedient Means," the second chapter, through "Prophecies Conferred on Learners and Adepts," the ninth chapter, predictions of enlightenment are bestowed on voice-hearers a total of four times.

Suda: The number of recipients gradually grows — starting with only Shariputra in the beginning and expanding to the four great voice-hearers, the five hundred disciples and, finally, the two thousand monks.

Ikeda: In "The Teacher of the Law," the scope of recipients expands further still.

Endo: Yes, up to that point, only voice-hearers had received prophecies of enlightenment. But in "The Teacher of the Law," Shakyamuni predicts enlightenment for all who delight for even a moment upon hearing a passage or verse of the Lotus Sutra. This, Shakyamuni says, is the only requirement for receiving the prophecy of enlightenment:

> Do you see in this great assembly the immeasurable number of heavenly beings, dragon kings, yakshas, gandharvas, asuras, garudas, kimnaras, mahoragas, human and nonhuman beings, as well as monks, nuns, laymen and laywomen, those who seek to become voice-hearers, who seek to become pratyekabuddhas, or who seek the Buddha way? Upon these various kinds of beings who …listen to one verse or one phrase of the Lotus Sutra of the Wonderful Law and for a moment think of it with joy I will bestow on all of them a prophecy that they will attain anuttara-samyak-sambodhi.[12] (LS10, 160–61)

Moreover, this is not limited to only those living in Shakyamuni's time. It also extends to people in the world after his passing.

Ikeda: It is a grand bestowal of prophecy, isn't it? It is a drama of the vital flowering of life.

Endo: There are still more predictions of Buddhahood in the Lotus Sutra. For example, in the "Devadatta" chapter, a prophecy of enlightenment is made for Devadatta, whom people thought could never attain Buddhahood because of the great evil he had committed. Also, in the "Encouraging Devotion" chapter, Shakyamuni makes a specific bestowal of prophecy of enlightenment for women. The teachings expounded before the Lotus Sutra held that women could not become Buddhas.

Ikeda: Ultimately, the Lotus Sutra predicts Buddhahood for all people. The bestowal of prophecy is one of a number of ways in which the central principle of the Lotus Sutra—that all living beings can attain the Buddha Way—is concretely expressed.

Saito: Among the many predictions of enlightenment, there are prophecies for those on a good path and prophecies for those on an evil path. While sutras other than the Lotus Sutra contain predictions of evil people such as Devadatta falling into hell, none predicts such people attaining Buddhahood. And while some sutras prophesy that evil persons will enter a good path, *pratyekabuddha* is the highest level they can hope to achieve.

Again, for the people of the two vehicles (voice-hearers and *pratyekabuddhas*), other sutras say that they have entered a path that will never lead to Buddhahood—that the goal of supreme enlightenment is denied to them eternally.

For this reason, the prophecies in the other sutras are termed "discriminatory."

Ikeda: The Lotus Sutra embodies the "bestowal of prophecy for all people" and the "equal bestowal of prophecy." It predicts Buddhahood for all, including those whom other sutras deny the possibility of attaining Buddhahood, people such as the voice-hearers and *pratyekabuddhas*, evil persons and women.

The requisites for receiving a prophecy of enlightenment are belief and understanding. In the words of "The Teacher of the Law" chapter, it means thinking for even a moment of one verse or phrase of the Lotus Sutra with joy. Joy is the engine that enables us to enter and advance along the path leading to Buddhahood.

Endo: Regarding the difference between the Lotus Sutra's predictions of enlightenment and those found in other sutras, T'ien-t'ai says: "In other sutras, prophecies of enlightenment are given only to bodhisattvas, and not to voice-hearers and *pratyekabuddhas*. They are given only to good persons and not to evil persons. They are given only to men and not to women. They are given only to human and heavenly beings and not to beings in the realm of Animality. In the Lotus Sutra, prophecies of enlightenment are given to all."[13]

The bestowal of prophecy of enlightenment upon all people is the heart of the Lotus Sutra.

Suda: In the *Profound Meaning of the Lotus Sutra*, T'ien-t'ai cites the reason for the centrality of the predictions of enlightenment for the voice-hearers in the Lotus Sutra as follows: "Doctrine expresses things clearly and in concrete form. Specific matters can be understood clearly through words. In the Lotus Sutra, specific prophecies are bestowed on the voice-hearers. This expresses the idea that all people can attain Buddhahood."[14]

These words specifically addressed to the voice-hearers clearly indicate that all people can attain Buddhahood. Since prophecies of enlightenment have been bestowed on even the voice-hearers —who, as persons of the two vehicles, were thought to be furthest from attaining Buddhahood—Shakyamuni's subsequent prediction of enlightenment for all people comes as no surprise.

Ikeda: The spirit of the Lotus Sutra's bestowal of prophecy is to enable all people to become Buddhas. It is probably Bodhisattva Never Disparaging who puts this spirit most directly into practice. This bodhisattva reveres all equally, telling them that he deeply respects them because in the future they will become Buddhas.

Saito: The words that Bodhisattva Never Disparaging speaks on approaching people are certainly a bestowal of prophecy. They constitute the so-called twenty-four–character Lotus Sutra:[15] "I have profound reverence for you, I would never dare treat you with disparagement or arrogance. Why? Because you are all practicing the bodhisattva way and are certain to attain Buddhahood" (LS20, 266–67).

Those whom Bodhisattva Never Disparaging salutes in this manner scorn him. They vilify, mock and attack him, retorting, in effect, "I don't need any false prophecy of enlightenment from a nobody like you!"

Endo: T'ien-t'ai interprets the prophecies of enlightenment in the Lotus Sutra in terms of the "three inherent potentials" of the Buddha nature. He says that the predictions of enlightenment made by Bodhisattva Never Disparaging represent the "bestowal of prophecy of innate Buddhahood."

The three inherent potentials of the Buddha nature are: (1) innate Buddhahood, the world of Buddhahood existing in all people; (2) the wisdom to perceive or express the world of Buddhahood; and (3) good actions, or practice, to develop this wisdom. These three potentials are the causes for attaining Buddhahood.

According to T'ien-t'ai, Shakyamuni's predictions of enlightenment in the Lotus Sutra for the voice-hearers represent the bestowal of prophecy of the wisdom to perceive the world of Buddhahood. The explanation that one can attain Buddhahood through the practice of praising the Buddha, as in the ten kinds of offerings[16] discussed in "The Teacher of the Law" chapter, T'ien-t'ai says, represents the "bestowal of prophecy of good actions or practice to develop this wisdom."

And, as I just mentioned, Bodhisattva Never Disparaging's perceiving the Buddha nature in all people and bowing to them in reverence correspond to the bestowal of prophecy of innate Buddhahood.

Saito: The bestowal of prophecy of innate Buddhahood means to cause people to awaken to the existence of the world of Buddhahood in their own lives.

Ikeda: Yes. The inherent potential of Buddhahood indicates one's heart and the inner realm of life itself. Therefore, causing people to awaken to the great potential of their lives corresponds to the bestowal of prophecy of innate Buddhahood.

Expressed more simply, it is to convey to each person: "You, too, will realize the greatest happiness without fail." It is to give hope and revive a spirit of challenge in the hearts of those who, mired in the darkness of suffering, have grown resigned and weary. In a stagnating and deadlocked society, it is to assert that human beings have the limitless potential to resolve all difficulties.

Each person is an entity of the Mystic Law. Each person is worthy of respect by virtue of his or her humanity. This is what Bodhisattva Never Disparaging reveals with his life through his practice of revering others. Nichiren Daishonin declared that his own practice is the same as that of Bodhisattva Never Disparaging. To chant and propagate Nam-myoho-renge-kyo is to bestow the prophecy of enlightenment in the Latter Day of the Law. The Daishonin says, "The word *prophecy* refers to Nam-myoho-renge-kyo" (GZ, 730).

Regarding this bestowal of prophecy through Nam-myoho-renge-kyo, he says, "It is the bestowal of prophecy of the Mystic Law, and therefore it is a bestowal of prophecy upon the Dharma-realm" (GZ, 731). "Bestowal of prophecy upon the Dharma-realm" means bestowal of prophecy upon all beings in the Ten Worlds. The bestowal of prophecy of Nam-myoho-renge-kyo indicates that all beings of the Ten Worlds are entities of the Mystic Law. To illustrate, even those in the world of Hell, because they are entities of the Mystic Law, definitely can attain Buddhahood. This is the Lotus Sutra's ultimate "bestowal of prophecy for all people" and "equal bestowal of prophecy."

Nichiren Daishonin's Buddhism is the Buddhism of sowing. Carrying out its bestowal of prophecy — Nam-myoho-renge-kyo — means planting the seed of the Mystic Law in people's lives and so enabling them to form a connection with the Mystic Law. It is to plant the realization in the depths of each person's life that he or she is an entity of the Mystic Law and to clarify the boundless potential of life.

Also, Nam-myoho-renge-kyo is the seed of happiness and

peace. The bestowal of prophecy of Nam-myoho-renge-kyo puts humankind on the sure path to happiness and peace. When the profound view of life and of human nature that all beings are entities of the Mystic Law takes root, humankind can advance along this sure path.

Buddhahood seems like a goal; but it is not. It is a clear path. It is hope itself—hope to advance eternally toward self-improvement, greater fulfillment and increased peace of mind and enjoyment in life. The future attainment of Buddhahood that the Lotus Sutra predicts teaches the attitude of focusing on the present and the future, the progressive spirit always to strive toward further growth and help more people become happy.

Endo: If Buddhahood meant achieving a state of perfection beyond which there was nothing else, wouldn't it be rather boring?

Ikeda: When we enter the path of Buddhahood, we can thoroughly enjoy from the depths of our being all of life's storms, blizzards and withering gales as well as, of course, its spring breezes, blue skies and sunshine; we attain the supreme state in which life is a joy and death is joyful, too. Following this path guarantees that we will experience such eternal fulfillment and hope.

In a sense, becoming a Buddha means continually actualizing the principles of 'attaining Buddhahood in this lifetime' and 'attaining Buddhahood in one's present form.'

Endo: The ultimate summation of these endeavors is the state of life of Nichiren Daishonin, who says, "When difficulties arise, we should regard these as 'joyful'" (GZ, 750).

Ikeda: I think that's correct. Encountering the 'three powerful enemies' of Buddhism and the 'three obstacles and four devils' is the greatest proof that we are advancing along the correct path. These obstacles assure us that if we can overcome these problems, then we can definitely attain Buddhahood.

Because we encounter obstacles, we know that the path of kosen-rufu on which we are advancing is correct. We can be confident that, in lifetime after lifetime, we will enter the path of Buddhahood. Obstacles are the source of the greatest encouragement.

Therefore, viewed from the perspective of faith, obstacles are also a "bestowal of prophecy." We could call them the final exam of our Buddhist practice. When the three powerful enemies vie with one another to attack us, we truly have the opportunity to enter the path of attaining Buddhahood. And once we enter that path, we will be Buddhas eternally.

For humankind, a correct path is indispensable. When I spoke with Dr. Aurelio Peccei, cofounder of The Club of Rome, we agreed modern civilization seemed to be hurtling out of control:

"We are driving at a reckless speed on a winding road."[17] "We are like a fearless child infatuated with the excitement of speed, stepping harder and harder on the accelerator of an automobile."[18] "We are...risking catastrophe at any moment."[19]

Endo: Knowing neither where we are headed nor in what direction we ought to go, we continue to career recklessly into impenetrable darkness without a sure path. That is the state of humankind today.

Ikeda: Since my dialogue with Dr. Peccei in the 1980s, this situation has not improved in the least. And I am deeply perplexed by the sense that recently even the energy to try to improve things seems in increasingly short supply.

Saito: It seems to me that the cause may lie in the fact that people have, in some sense, been "left behind." Machines have advanced in both power and speed. And although the "automobile" of a civilized society that brings together the fruits of this progress has been created, the people who must sit in the driver's seat have not themselves matured to the point where they can properly fulfill that role. As a result, it is as though children are causing the automobile of society to career out of control and are thrilling at the speed.

Ikeda: That's right. How can we reduce the speed of this out-of-control vehicle and point humanity in the right direction?

This is only possible through human revolution—a revolution in the life of each individual. This was the conclusion that Dr. Peccei and I reached. People themselves have to change. We have to foster people who can "put themselves on the right track."[20] It stands to reason that as the number of such people in society increases, the direction of society will also change. Peccei remarked, "The human revolution is the key to positive action leading to the adoption of a new course and the revival of human fortunes."[21]

Buddhism cultivates in people the ability to put themselves on the right track. The right track could be taken as meaning the path leading to happiness for both oneself and others. We are entering the sure path toward that goal ourselves and helping others to do the same; this endeavor to provide inspiration and hope is the movement of human revolution. It is the movement for peace, culture and education based on Buddhism, which we in the SGI are promoting. In a broad sense, this accords with the spirit of the bestowal of prophecy in the Lotus Sutra.

DISCUSSION MEETINGS ARE JOYFUL FORUMS FOR THE "BESTOWAL OF PROPHECY"

Suda: In that light, SGI discussion meetings take on increased significance. Discussion meetings are forums for human revolution; they are the very forefront of our efforts to provide people with the hope and inspiration to live life to the fullest.

Ikeda: Precisely. That's exactly what I would like to stress.

President Makiguchi designated these gatherings "discussion meetings to prove experimentally the life of major good." This means, in other words, showing through actual proof—in a manner that anyone can accept and understand—the wonder of "faith manifesting itself in daily life," which we experience when we base ourselves on the Mystic Law and the wonder of human revolution—a way of life dedicated to the good of society and the well-being of others. Moreover, from the outset, the Soka Gakkai and SGI discussion meetings have been open to people from all walks of life.

SGI discussion meetings are grass-roots forums that provide society with wisdom and vitality.

On hearing others' experiences of benefit, people renew their determinations: "They fought hard and won. I, too, can change my destiny. I will give it my best effort!"

And people encourage fellow members who are struggling amid various obstacles: "Let's try to grow, just like this person! Let's make this person our model!"

The give-and-take at discussion meetings encourages and reassures people that they can attain Buddhahood in this lifetime and arouses in them a sense of mission for kosen-rufu. In that sense, it has the same effect as the predictions of enlightenment in the Lotus Sutra. We could say, therefore, that discussion meetings are "forums for the bestowal of prophecy" where children of the Buddha encourage and are encouraged by one another.

Suda: This is similar to the significance of the commendations awarded to members who have made important contributions to kosen-rufu that we talked about earlier.

Ikeda: Yes. Having the spirit to praise others makes us worthy of praise ourselves.

I want to add one more thing. It was in Shimoda, in Izu, where he had gone to attend a discussion meeting, that President Makiguchi was arrested. At the time, during World War II, discussion meetings were held under the supervision of Special Higher Police. And though he had been harassed many times because of his refusal to accept the Shinto talisman, Mr. Makiguchi did not retreat a single step. The discussion meeting for him was thus also the harsh battlefield for a spiritual struggle against the country's militarist authorities.

We can also view Nichiren Daishonin's struggle for religious reformation as having begun with gatherings for dialogue comparable to the discussion meetings we hold today.

Saito: While the Daishonin was in exile, his followers gathered to read his letters, and this gave them the strength to overcome great adversity. I think that these gatherings for mutual encouragement could also be termed discussion meetings.

Ikeda: Since the time of Nichiren Daishonin, therefore, and the time of presidents Makiguchi and Toda, a spirit of great struggle has been part and parcel of the tradition of the discussion meeting. Great significance attaches to our efforts to cause this spirit to flow in abundance and make each discussion meeting joyful and bright.

In a directionless age, we are blazing a solid path toward human happiness. I hope this strength and optimism, to survive and triumph over any difficulty, will pulse in the great discussion meeting movement, spreading from the heart of one person to another.

NOTES

1. *Toda Josei Zenshu* (Collected Works of Josei Toda) (Tokyo: Seikyo Shimbunsha, 1985), vol. 4, p. 422.

2. Ibid., p. 474.

3. Also known as Mahakashyapa.

4. Also known as Mahakatyayana.

5. This parable concerns the replacement of the three vehicles of the voice-hearers, *pratyekabuddhas* (people of Learning and Realization) and bodhisattvas with the one Buddha vehicle.

6. Five elements: The five constituents of all things in the universe, according to ancient Indian belief. They are earth, water, fire, wind and space. The first four correspond respectively to the physical states of solid, liquid, heat and gas. Space is interpreted as integrating the other four elements.

7. Jambunada Gold: Gold found in the river running through the forest of the Jambu trees in Jambudvipa.

8. Tamalapatra: The leaf of the tamala, which is a kind of sandalwood tree.

9. For further discussion of this point, please refer to previous chapters in this series.

10. Zuiryu Nakamura, *Gendaigo yaku hokekyo jo* (modern translation of The Lotus Sutra, Part 1) (Tokyo: Shunjusha, 1995), p. 132.

11. Jetavana Monastery: A monastery in Shravasti where Shakyamuni is said to have lived and taught during the rainy season for the last twenty-five years of his life. It was built as an offering by Sudatta on land provided by Prince Jetri. Along with the Bamboo Grove Monastery in Rajagriha, it was one of the two major centers of the Buddha's propagation activities.

12. Anuttara-samyak-sambodhi: Supreme perfect enlightenment, the enlightenment of a Buddha.

13. *Words and Phrases of the Lotus Sutra*, vol. 7

14. *Profouns Meaning of the Lotus Sutra*, vol. 6.

15. Twenty-four-character Lotus Sutra: Words that Bodhisattva Never Disparaging spoke to all people; in Chinese, they comprise twenty-four characters, hence the name.

16. Ten kinds of offerings: Presenting various offerings of flowers, incense, necklaces, powdered incense, paste incense, incense for burning, silken canopies, streamers and banners, clothing and music, and pressing their palms together in reverence.

17. Aurelio Peccei and Daisaku Ikeda, *Before It Is Too Late* (New York: Kodansha International Ltd., 1984), p. 148.

18. Ibid., pp. 125–26.

19. Ibid., p. 148.

20. Ibid., p. 152.

21. Ibid.

PART FIVE

"The Parable of the Phantom City" Chapter

5   The Eternal Bond of Mentor and Disciple

Suda: Recently, I heard a member say that the world today is in a pitiful state. Politicians shirk responsibility and spend all their time just trying to protect their own positions. This member felt that jealousy and irresponsibility, apathy and heartlessness reign, and that with the country in such straits, can very many be passionately devoted to high ideals?

Ikeda: I think many people share these sentiments. In 1846, the great Danish philosopher Soren Kierkegaard wrote in *The Present Age,* "Our age is essentially one of understanding and reflection, without passion, momentarily bursting into enthusiasm, and shrewdly relapsing into repose."[1] He might just as well have been describing the situation in the world today.

Endo: An age when people lack passion and are turned inward will be dominated by jealousy. Once this tendency is firmly rooted in people's lives, they will try to pull down anyone who is outstanding in an attempt to level the human geography, as it were. This is the essence of Kierkegaard's argument.

Ikeda: It was not until more than half a century after Kierkegaard's death that people in other countries began to pay attention to his ideas. Many thinkers hailed his writings as prophetic; German philosopher Karl Jaspers, for example, marveled, "It's as though it was written yesterday."[2]

What gave Kierkegaard such profound insight into the problems of modern society? One reason, I think, is that he was convinced his life would be short, and so he struggled to accomplish everything he could in his limited span of years.

Endo: Armed with his pen, he stood up to the authoritarian clerics of his day and the libelous accusations made against him in the press. Never relenting in his struggles, he died at forty-two.

Ikeda: Kierkegaard believed that he would not live to be thirty-four. His mother had died young, and he had lost five of his six siblings; two elder sisters, who lived comparatively long lives, died at thirty-three. He felt certain that he would not outlive these older sisters.

When he reached his thirty-fourth birthday, he wrote in his diary that it was "astonishing" and "incomprehensible" that he had survived to this age.[3]

In just over a decade, mostly in his thirties, he published approximately forty works. As many as twenty more volumes of his writings were published posthumously. In his book *The Present Age*, he concludes that the only way to stave off the "leveling" of modern society is for individuals to attain immovable "religious courage."[4] Kierkegaard's philosophy consistently returns to the point that people have to know their mission in life, that they need to discover an ideal to which they can dedicate their lives and for which they would be willing to die.

Saito: The ability to awaken people to such an ideal and such a sense of mission will be one of the prime requirements of religion in the twenty-first century.

Ikeda: That wisdom is the Lotus Sutra's gift to present and future generations. "Why was I born in this world?" "What do I need to accomplish in this life?" The Buddha appeared in this world to help people come to grips with these universal questions.

In "Expedient Means," the second chapter of the Lotus Sutra,

Shakyamuni first expounds the truth to which he has become enlightened. At that juncture, only Shariputra grasps his meaning. In the following chapter, the Buddha relates various similes and parables that enable the four great voice-hearer disciples to gain understanding. But the Buddha has to open the eyes of still more people. Toward that end, he expounds "The Parable of the Phantom City," the seventh chapter, which further dramatizes the great illuminating force of the Buddha's wisdom.

THE MENTOR–DISCIPLE RELATIONSHIP ORIGINATES IN THE DISTANT PAST

> "At that time the leader, knowing that the people have become rested and are no longer fearful or weary, wipes out the phantom city and says to the group, 'You must go now. The place where the treasure is is close by. That great city of a while ago was a mere phantom that I conjured up so that you could rest.'
>
> "Monks, the Thus Come One is in a similar position. He is now acting as a great leader for you. He knows that the bad road of birth and death and earthly desires is steep, difficult, long and far-stretching, but that it must be traveled, it must be passed over." (LS7, 136)

Saito: The key concept in "Phantom City" is "causes and conditions."

Endo: This term, which indicates a karmic relationship, is still part of the vocabulary of the Japanese language today; but the Buddhist meaning seems to have been lost, and instead it has rather negative connotations, such as an undesirable fate. This is of course not the original meaning of the term in Buddhism.

Saito: The karmic relationship described in "Phantom City" is the profound connection that has existed from past lives between

Shakyamuni and his voice-hearer disciples. This chapter, in other words, expounds the bond of mentor and disciple.

In the Sanskrit text of the Lotus Sutra, this chapter is titled "Relations From Past Lives" (Skt Purva-yoga). And in the Sho-hokke-kyo,[5] a Chinese translation of the sutra by Dharmaraksha, the chapter is called "Distant Past," because it explains the distant past of major world system dust particle *kalpas*. Kumarajiva named the chapter "The Parable of the Phantom City" because of the well-known parable related in its latter half.

Ikeda: Not only had Shakyamuni Buddha taught the voice-hearers in his present life, he had instructed them tirelessly and ceaselessly since the remote past. This chapter explains the karmic relationship existing between them since that distant time.

"Our relationship is not limited to this lifetime alone," Shakyamuni tells them in effect. "I have been together with you all along." It is this impassioned message that enables the voice-hearers to awaken to the truth.

They are deeply moved. They realize that the teachings of the two vehicles (for voice-hearers and *pratyekabuddhas*), producing only partial enlightenment, were an expedient means, a mere "phantom city." And that the "treasure land" of Buddhahood was the true destination all along. They understand that their mentor, Shakyamuni, guided them with such strong forbearance, such profound mercy and such great skill to bring them along with him to this treasure land. This is the significance of the parable.

Suda: "The Parable of the Phantom City," it would seem, is an apt title for the chapter.

Major world system dust particle *kalpas*, which is used to explain the duration of the relationship between mentor and disciple, is a period of staggering length. In "Phantom City," this concept is explained as follows. Suppose someone reduces all the lands in a major world system to dust and then, traveling eastward, drops one particle of dust each time he passes a thousand worlds. He continues in this way until he has disposed of the entire mass of particles. If the person then reduces to dust all the worlds he has passed, whether or not they received a dust particle, and if each particle signifies one *kalpa*[6] or aeon, major world system dust particles *kalpas* is the length of time corresponding to the total number of dust particles.

The particles are in fact too numerous to be counted. The text speaks of first reducing a major world system to dust. In ancient Indian cosmology, a major world system could be compared to, in modern terms, a galaxy so vast as to include a billion solar systems. The time unit "*kalpa*" is also unfathomably long.

I wonder why it's necessary to go back to such a remote time to clarify a karmic relationship.

Endo: On that point, the Great Teacher T'ien-t'ai of China says that, in "Phantom City," the "process of instruction is revealed from beginning to end." The "beginning" is the remote past, the "end" is the present of the Lotus Sutra.

Ikeda: The key lies in the beginning. If we understand what happened then, we can also understand Shakyamuni's meaning when he preached the one supreme Buddha vehicle in the Lotus Sutra, which is the teaching for attaining enlightenment.

The initial planting of the seed is extremely important. Nichiren Daishonin says:

"The relationship between Shakyamuni Buddha and his disciples can be traced back to the time when, as the sixteenth son of the Buddha Great Universal Wisdom Excellence, he planted the seeds of Buddhahood in their lives…. Ordinary people and the persons of the two vehicles came to the Lotus Sutra gradually through the first four flavors of teachings. They then revealed the seeds of Buddhahood from within themselves and were able to obtain the fruit of enlightenment" (WND, 368).

The seeds are sown, they mature, and at last fruit is produced. In terms of this process, Shakyamuni is now about to lead the voice-hearers to the final stage of fruition, or attainment of Buddhahood, by bestowing on them prophecies of enlightenment. But before doing so, he teaches them the significance of the sowing of the seed at the beginning.

What sort of period, then, was the time of sowing? What were the circumstances under which Shakyamuni began giving instruction? Why don't we try first to give an overview of the contents of "Phantom City"?

Saito: This chapter starts by explaining the appearance in the distant past of a Buddha named Great Universal Wisdom Excellence. The land of this Buddha is called Well Constituted and his *kalpa*, Great Form. From these names, we get a sense of the character of the age.

Great Universal Wisdom Excellence, as his name suggests, possessed penetrating mystic powers and perfect wisdom. Great Form, the name of the *kalpa*, means excellent in appearance. And Well Constituted, the name of the land, means begun or initiated well.

Ikeda: The appearance in the world of a great spiritual leader such as the Buddha Great Universal Wisdom Excellence probably signaled the dawn of a wondrous new age; it marked a time of beginning.

Spiritual reformers are sure to appear at the beginning of a new age. These people themselves develop a new dimension of spirituality and liberate the hearts of those caught up in outmoded ways of thinking. Again, they may exert an intangible yet profound spiritual influence on people.

Let us of the SGI always advance with the pride of pioneers. Nichiren Daishonin says, "The votaries who chant Nam-myoho-renge-kyo are the Buddha Great Universal Wisdom Excellence" (GZ, 733).

Suda: "Phantom City" explains the attainment of Buddhahood by Great Universal Wisdom Excellence in considerable detail.

What I find difficult to understand here is why it says that, even after he had seated himself in the place of practice and defeated powerful devilish forces, he still did not attain Buddhahood for ten *kalpas*. The sutra states:

> This Buddha at first sat in the place of practice and, hav-
> ing smashed the armies of the devil, was on the point
> of attaining anuttara-samyak-sambodhi [supreme
> enlightenment], but the doctrines of the Buddhas did
> not appear before him. This state continued for one
> small kalpa, and so on for ten small kalpas, the Buddha
> sitting with legs crossed, body and mind unmoving, but
> the doctrines of the Buddhas still did not appear before
> him. (LS7, 119)

Ikeda: The statement that he "smashed the armies of the devil" is taken to mean that he had fundamentally conquered earthly desires. But simply overcoming earthly desires is not in itself attaining enlightenment. It is one aspect of enlightenment. True enlightenment is inseparable from the compassion and wisdom to lead people to happiness.

"Phantom City" is expounded for the voice-hearers. The voice-hearers suppose that enlightenment means extinguishing earthly desires and entering a state of perfect calm and tranquillity. It may be that Shakyamuni describes Great Universal Wisdom Excellence's Buddhahood in this way to indicate to the voice-hearers that conquering earthly desires does not in itself constitute attaining the Buddha's true enlightenment.

Compassion, wisdom and earthly desires, of course, belong to the realm of the intangible, of nonsubstantiality, and they should not be viewed in a phenomenal sense. On that premise, to put it simply, the Buddha's enlightenment lies not in "eradicating" earthly desires but rather in infusing them with compassion and wisdom. It is a matter of changing the turbid river of earthly desires, karma and suffering into a pure stream of compassion and wisdom, of turning the negative waves of life into waves of goodness.

Those who achieve this possess a perfectly tranquil and serene state of life in the sense that they are not troubled by earthly desires; at the same time, their lives have a vigorous dynamism. The Buddha's state of life is like the ocean. No matter what turmoil there may be on the surface, in its depths there is absolute calm and tranquillity. And the Buddha's life constantly pulses with "waves of goodness." The Buddha is called the Thus Come One because the workings of the Mystic Law "come thus," or manifest purely and directly, in his life.

This is the Buddha's enlightenment in perfect unification with the Mystic Law.

Endo: I find it interesting in this chapter that heavenly beings continuously make offerings to Great Universal Wisdom Excellence during that interval of ten *kalpas* before he has attained Buddhahood. The beings of the Trayastrimsha heaven make an offering of a grand lion seat, the Brahma kings cause heavenly flowers to rain down continuously, and the Four Heavenly Kings constantly beat on heavenly drums. It could be said that these beings are like cheerleaders urging him on in his efforts to attain supreme enlightenment.

Ikeda: In becoming cheerleaders for the Buddha, these heavenly beings, who represent all living beings, express people's spirit of longing for the Buddha to appear. In a broad sense, the Brass Band, Fife and Drum Corps, and all the chorus or music groups of the SGI, are cheerleaders to urge us on in our individual attainment of Buddhahood and in our efforts to accomplish kosen-rufu. While we might think of the Buddhist deities as inhabiting some distant realm, they are in fact close at hand.

Endo: When Great Universal Wisdom Excellence finally attains supreme enlightenment, the entire world is filled with a brilliant light surpassing that of the sun and moon.

Ikeda: The Mystic Law thoroughly permeates the Buddha's life, and the fragrance of the Buddha's vast compassion and infinite wisdom to lead people to enlightenment pervades the universe. This, I think, is what this light signifies.

THE RESTATEMENT
OF THE BUDDHA'S TEACHING

Suda: Next, the sixteen princes appear. These are children of Great Universal Wisdom Excellence from before he had renounced the world. The sixteenth of these sons is Shakyamuni in a previous incarnation. Learning that their father has become a Buddha, the princes approach him and entreat him to expound the Law.

In addition to the sixteen sons, the Brahma kings in the worlds throughout the universe in the ten directions —north, south, east, west, northwest, northeast, southeast, southwest, up and down— also unanimously beseech Great Universal Wisdom Excellence to expound the Law. The sutra describes in detail this event, known as the "appeal of the Brahma kings," which takes place on a truly colossal scale.

The text specifically mentions four Brahma kings named Save All, Great Compassion, Wonderful Law and Shikhin. Shikhin is the name of a leading Brahma king, but none of the others appears in standard Indian mythology. Save All, Great Compassion and Wonderful Law may represent the spirit of yearning for the appearance of a Buddha who will widely and compassionately expound the Mystic Law to lead people to happiness.

Ikeda: That's probably so. Before the appearance of Great Universal Wisdom Excellence, people's lives were filled with suffering, and the age had reached a deadlock. The sutra describes people's plight, saying "from darkness they enter darkness" (LS7, 121). In the depths of their lives, people yearned for the appearance of a Buddha who would put an end to the negative spiral described as "from darkness to darkness." These names express that spirit.

President Toda often said:"In commerce or in any other sphere, what people are seeking will catch on and spread. Kosen-rufu can definitely be accomplished in this age because people now seek the Mystic Law."

Endo: In response to the requests of the sixteen princes and the Brahma kings, Great Universal Wisdom Excellence begins expounding the Law. He first explains the doctrines of the four noble truths and the twelve-linked chain of causation. By mastering this partial truth, many people achieve the state of voice-hearer.

But the sixteen princes are not satisfied with those doctrines, and they implore the Buddha to expound the true cause of his enlightenment.

Ikeda: The four noble truths and the twelve-linked chain of causation are provisional teachings that reveal only one aspect of the Buddha's enlightenment. Various things can be said about these doctrines; but essentially, their basic point is that people can gain a state of peace and tranquillity by extinguishing earthly desires, which are understood to be the cause of suffering. But the Buddha's true intention is to enable people to acquire the unsurpassed enlightenment that he himself has attained. And so, at the request of the sixteen princes, and after awaiting the proper time, the Buddha expounds the Lotus Sutra, clarifying that intention.

Saito: The sutra says that after Great Universal Wisdom Excellence has expounded the Lotus Sutra for a period of eight thousand *kalpas*, he goes into meditation for a period of eighty-four thousand *kalpas*. During and after his meditation, the sixteen princes, who have become bodhisattvas, expound the Lotus Sutra just as their father had. This is known as the "restatement of the teaching of Great Universal Wisdom Excellence." It is called a restatement because they reiterate the Lotus Sutra that the Buddha, their mentor, had expounded.

Ikeda: Great Universal Wisdom Excellence and the sixteen princes all taught the same Lotus Sutra. The sixteen princes truly followed the path of oneness of mentor and disciple.

Suda: As bodhisattvas, the sixteen princes expounded the Lotus Sutra, each instructing countless beings. These beings were then reborn in the lands of various Buddhas together with the bodhisattvas who were their teachers, their mentors, and from whom they then received further instruction. In a well-known passage, the sutra says that they "dwelled here and there in various Buddha lands, constantly reborn in company with their teachers" (LS7, 140).

Endo: At the end of "Phantom City," Shakyamuni reveals that he is the sixteenth prince, and that the voice-hearers who are his disciples at present and those who will appear after his passing are the beings he began instructing at that time. Shakyamuni addresses the voice-hearers, saying:

> I myself was numbered among the sixteen
> and in the past preached for you.
> For this reason I will employ an expedient means
> to lead you in the pursuit of the Buddha wisdom;
> because of these earlier causes and conditions
> I now preach the Lotus Sutra.
> I will cause you to enter the Buddha way.... (LS7, 140)

Here, reference is made to the "causes and conditions" from previous lives linking Shakyamuni and the voice-hearers. Purna, Ananda and the other voice-hearers who could not grasp the meaning of the Buddha's preaching in the "Expedient Means" or "Simile and Parable" chapters, attain the way for the first time when they hear Shakyamuni's explanation of their karmic relationship here in "Phantom City." And in the subsequent "Prophecy of Enlightenment for Five Hundred Disciples," the eighth chapter, and "Prophecies Conferred on Learners and Adepts," the ninth chapter, they receive prophecies of their future attainment of Buddhahood.

Ikeda: The unfathomably profound bond between Shakyamuni and the voice-hearers has now been clarified. The origin of this bond is their having heard Shakyamuni expound the Lotus Sutra in the distant past, at the time of the restatement of the teaching of the Buddha Great Universal Wisdom Excellence.

Saito: In other words, that's when the seed of Buddhahood was sown in their lives.

Ikeda: Precisely. At that time, the voice-hearers heard the Lotus Sutra and conceived the desire in the depths of their lives to attain the same unsurpassed enlightenment as the Buddha Great Universal Wisdom Excellence. They aroused a seeking mind. Thus, in the "Five Hundred Disciples" chapter, the voice-hearers say:

> Through the long night the World-Honored One
> constantly in his pity teaches and converts us,
> causing us to plant the seeds of an unsurpassed
> aspiration. (LS8, 152)

Saito: At the same time as the seed of enlightenment is planted in their lives, they conceive an "unsurpassed aspiration."

Ikeda: "Unsurpassed aspiration" means a desire to attain the Buddha's unsurpassed enlightenment. That this enlightenment can in fact be attained is also part of the Lotus Sutra. Since the Buddha's unsurpassed enlightenment is the manifestation of his compassion and wisdom to save people, this aspiration is informed by the wish to lead all beings to enlightenment just as the Buddha does.

Saito: Elsewhere in the same chapter, Purna says, "Only the Buddha, the World-Honored One, is capable of knowing the wish that we have had deep in our hearts from the start" (LS8, 144). The wish "deep in our hearts" is the original aspiration that the disciples have cherished in the depths of their lives. It seems to me that the desire to attain unsurpassed enlightenment and to lead all beings to happiness is an aspiration that, fundamentally, all people possess.

Ikeda: Isn't that what we call the Buddha nature? The term *Buddha nature* does not appear in the Lotus Sutra. But it seems that this is what original aspiration in the depths of one's life indicates.

Suda: Understanding the causes and conditions that existed in the past, then, in essence means understanding the aspiration—the Buddha nature—in the depths of one's being.

Ikeda: Stated more simply, this fundamental wish could be described as an aspiration or desire for the happiness of oneself and others. The very simplicity of this might seem anticlimactic, since it's something that all people understand on some level; but making this one's guiding and fundamental spirit is in fact extremely difficult. This is because hindrances in the form of earthly desires, ignorance, greed, egoism and divisiveness prevent people from doing so.

To base our lives thoroughly on this spirit, therefore, we need a teacher, a mentor, who can guide us in the right direction. It seems that this is what the "Phantom City" chapter teaches through the elucidation of the karmic causes and conditions linking mentor and disciple over an extremely long time.

In short, "causes and conditions" indicates the eternal bonds that form between people. These bonds certainly do not exist apart from human beings, nor do they fetter or bind people externally.

On the contrary, the disciples themselves perceive the cause for attaining Buddhahood at the core of their being. That is, they recollect their original aspiration. Also, they awaken to a sense of gratitude for the condition provided by their mentor—that is, for their relationship with him—in helping them develop this cause for the effect of Buddhahood. This sense of appreciation and excitement at realizing this supreme bond with the mentor is the spirit of "Phantom City."

Saito: T'ien-t'ai says of the "one great reason [lit. cause and condition]" for which all Buddhas make their appearance in the world: "Living beings possess the capacity to respond to the Buddhas; so this is called the 'cause.' The Buddhas, observing this capacity, act in response to it; so this is called the 'condition.'"[7] He indicates that the "cause" rests with the disciples (i.e., living beings), while the "condition" rests with the Buddha.

Ikeda: Yes. And of cause and condition, cause is naturally primary. Conditions function to support and assist the cause. In the path of mentor and disciple, too, the awareness of the disciple is primary. The response of the mentor depends on the strength of the disciple's seeking spirit, sense of responsibility and determination.

That said, the Buddha industriously teaches and guides his disciples over past, present and future, never abandoning any of them. He educates them and embraces them in his mercy. It seems to me that the Buddha's immense compassion is the main point the Lotus Sutra seeks to convey.

The disciples believe in and seek out the mentor, and the mentor protects and trains the disciples. The mentor, ultimately, does not abandon even disciples who have forgotten their pledge. This most beautiful of human bonds is the relationship of mentor and disciple in Buddhism.

Saito: The mentor–disciple relationship in Buddhism is neither a one-way relationship from the mentor above to the disciple below nor is it an oppressive, feudalistic type of master–servant relationship.

Endo: If I may digress, Karel Dobbelaere, former president of the International Society of Religion, citing the profound ties between our successive presidents, has observed that the Soka Gakkai is pervaded by the mentor–disciple relationship. He also feels that the Soka Gakkai's unity, built on these human bonds of mentor and disciple, provides members with a great deal of guidance and direction. In other words, he sees that human bonds constitute the very nucleus of the SGI.

Ikeda: That's keen insight. "The 'cause and condition' for our appearance in this world," President Toda declared, "is to hoist up the great flag of kosen-rufu."[8] That's the raison d'etre of the SGI organization. And the essence of this organization is the mentor–disciple relationship.

In Buddhism, therefore, mentor and disciple are comrades advancing together toward the common objective of kosen-rufu, toward the creation of a world where Buddhist ideals and principles are widely embraced. The mentor–disciple relationship is an extension of the kind that exists between those with greater experience in life or in faith and those with lesser. In one sense, mentor and disciple stand face to face. Yet on a more fundamental level, mentor and disciple are comrades standing side by side.

Endo: It is a bond that absolutely cannot be broken. In this connection, Mr. Toda, reminiscing about his mentor—the first Soka Gakkai president, Tsunesaburo Makiguchi—once said:

> I explain the persecution that I underwent on account of the Lotus Sutra [during which I was imprisoned for two years] with the following passage from the ["Phantom City" chapter of the] Lotus Sutra: "[They] dwelled here and there in various Buddha lands, constantly reborn in company with their teachers" (LS7, 140).
>
> "Reborn in company with" indicates that, through the beneficial power of the Lotus Sutra, mentor and

disciple will definitely be born together at the same time, and will together study the Lotus Sutra. All we [Mr. Makiguchi and I] did was put into practice this rule that has existed for countless millions of aeons.

Our relationship as mentor and disciple is not limited to this lifetime alone. When I am the mentor, President Makiguchi becomes the disciple; and when President Makiguchi is the mentor, I become the disciple. We are inseparable companions in both the past and the future.[9]

Suda: At Mr. Makiguchi's third memorial in November 1946, President Toda said:

In your vast and boundless mercy, you took me with you even to prison. Thanks to that, I could read with my life the Lotus Sutra passage, "[they] dwelled here and there in various Buddha lands, constantly reborn in company with their teachers." As a result of that benefit, I could understand the true meaning of the teaching of the Bodhisattvas of the Earth and could, albeit only dimly, grasp the meaning of the Lotus Sutra with my life. What great happiness this is!

A certain Japanese religious scholar was deeply impressed by these words, which he said expressed the very essence of Mr. Toda's religious encounter.

Saito: At a time when other disciples bore grudges against Mr. Makiguchi and condemned him for having provoked the persecution, President Toda alone expressed gratitude to his mentor for having allowed him to accompany him to prison.

Ikeda: When we become aware of this indestructible bond of mentor and disciple, limitless power wells forth. Our lives well with boundless hope, infinite mercy and inexhaustible wisdom.

To Shijo Kingo, who had accompanied the Daishonin during the Tatsunokuchi Persecution and been prepared to die at his mentor's side, Nichiren Daishonin wrote: "If you should fall into hell for some grave offense, no matter how Shakyamuni Buddha might urge me to become a Buddha, I would refuse; I would rather go to hell with you. For if you and I should fall into hell together, we would find Shakyamuni Buddha and the Lotus Sutra there" (WND, 850).

Learning of this supreme bond of mentor and disciple in "Phantom City," Shakyamuni's disciples finally recall their own original aspiration, and their fundamental mission. In doing so, they finally enter the path of attaining Buddhahood. They have received a bestowal of prophecy that they will attain enlightenment.

Before that point, when they heard Shakyamuni talk about the truth to which he became enlightened in the "Expedient Means" chapter or relate allegories in "Simile and Parable," it had seemed to them that the Buddha's teaching concerned other people or matters external to themselves. But now they suddenly realize, "This is about me personally!" "The Buddha is explaining my own situation!" This is a key point.

In President Toda's day, virtually all Soka Gakkai members were poor. But Mr. Toda, with great persistence, repeatedly taught these people, who were widely derided as a "gathering of the poor and sick": "You yourselves are the Bodhisattvas of the Earth whom the Lotus Sutra describes." He praised the members as "emissaries of the Buddha" and even "emanations of the Daishonin." "Aren't ordinary people most worthy of respect?" he proclaimed. "Aren't you and I, the members of the Soka Gakkai, the most noble personages of all?"[10]

Those who developed the confidence that they possessed a mission from the remote past advanced together with their mentor on the great path of kosen-rufu. This is the path for attaining Buddhahood. And by following this path, they recalled and awakened to their own original aspiration from the distant past.

Since "Phantom City" is in the theoretical teaching, or first half, of the Lotus Sutra, it is of limited depth. Nonetheless, I feel its significance lies in teaching the disciples that each of them is a protagonist in the grand and eternal drama of mentor and disciple.

The Parable of the Phantom City and the Treasure Land

Saito: After explaining the karmic relationship linking him and his present disciples, Shakyamuni relates the parable of the phantom city and the treasure land.

Suda: In the parable, a caravan traveling through the desert, guided by a single leader, is undertaking a long and hazardous journey of five hundred *yojanas* to a land of treasures. Along the way, however, the people in the caravan become extremely weary and disheartened, and they tell the leader they cannot go any further.

Were they to turn back, all their efforts up to that point would be in vain. The leader pities the people for wanting to return and give up the wonderful treasure. So when they have traveled more than three hundred *yojanas*, he uses his transcendental powers to create a great city; and he urges the people on, telling them that when they enter the city they can enjoy peace and tranquillity. The people rejoice upon hearing this, and they proceed ahead to the city, where they rest their thoroughly exhausted bodies and recoup their strength.

After they have had sufficient rest, the leader makes the city disappear. He then tells the people that the city was nothing more than an illusion he had conjured up to allow them to rest, and that their true destination, the treasure land, is close at hand (cf. LS7, 140–41).

The phantom city that the leader shows them corresponds to the expedient teachings of the three vehicles the Buddha expounds to guide people toward enlightenment. The treasure land represents the one Buddha vehicle toward which people should ultimately aim.

Specifically, this parable clarifies that the level of awakening achieved by the voice-hearers and *pratyekabuddhas* (which corresponds to the phantom city) is an expedient means, and that the Buddha's unsurpassed enlightenment (the treasure land) is the true enlightenment toward which they should exclusively direct their efforts.

Endo: This is a metaphor that is easy to understand and that one can readily visualize. The disciples had grown content with the teachings of the three vehicles. But the Buddha refutes their willingness to be satisfied with a low state of life and points them toward the true objective of the one Buddha vehicle. In the parable, this is expressed by his provisionally creating the phantom city and then causing it to disappear.

Ikeda: Yes, but that's only the surface meaning of the parable. From the text of the Lotus Sutra, we gather that the leader makes the phantom city disappear and that they then proceed to the treasure land. But Nichiren Daishonin goes beyond this interpretation, explaining that the phantom city and the treasure land, rather than being distinct, are in fact inseparable.

Suda: In the "Record of the Orally Transmitted Teachings," we find the following passage:

> The Ten Worlds are all of them phantom cities, and each of these Ten Worlds is a treasure land.
>
> Or again, the phantom city is the nine worlds other than Buddhahood, and the treasure land is the state of Buddhahood. The distance to the treasure land by way of the phantom city is five hundred *yojanas*. This distance of five hundred *yojanas* is symbolic of the illusions of thought and desire, of the dusts and sands that impede

Buddhist practice, and of darkness or ignorance. The five hundred *yojanas* of earthly desires, in essence, indicate the five characters of the Mystic Law; this means that the phantom city is identical to the treasure land. In the statement that the phantom city is identical to the treasure land, "identical to" indicates Nam-myoho-renge-kyo. Each life-moment in the phantom city is a life-moment in the treasure land. (GZ, 732)

Saito: When we view the phantom city and the treasure land as existing separately as "expedient means" and "truth," respectively, the former becomes a "means" and the latter, the "end." Consequently, we think of using a means to arrive at the end. On the other hand, when we view the phantom city and the treasure land as one and the same, the means includes the end.

Endo: If we view the end and the means as distinct, then the means becomes secondary and value resides exclusively in the end. Also, from this standpoint, we may tend to feel that, as long as the end can be attained, then the means whereby people arrive there is unimportant.

Ikeda: If the world of Buddhahood is the "end" or objective, then the nine worlds become the "process" leading to it. The view that we only arrive at Buddhahood after escaping the nine worlds implies discontinuity between the nine worlds and the world of Buddhahood—in other words, that the nine worlds do not contain the world of Buddhahood, and vice versa. But, as indicated in the above passage of the "Orally Transmitted Teachings," the idea that we attain enlightenment only after eradicating 'the three categories of illusion' is the way of thinking of the provisional, pre-Lotus Sutra teachings.

Shakyamuni's true intention in expounding the Lotus Sutra was to clarify that the nine worlds contain the world of Buddhahood and that the expedient means are themselves the truth.

Accordingly, the phantom city and the treasure land are not separate or distinct. The phantom city is identical to the treasure land.

From this perspective, the process is, in actuality, the end. In other words, the attainment of Buddhahood is not a destination at the end of the road of Buddhist practice. Rather, the actions of someone who practices and spreads Buddhism are themselves the actions of the Buddha.

Suda: This is the principle to which Nichikan refers when he says, "Buddhahood means a strong mind of faith in the Lotus Sutra."

Ikeda: Yes. The Buddha is not some nonhuman or superhuman being who dwells apart from this world. Nichiren Daishonin says, "The Buddha is in fact the living beings of the nine worlds" (GZ, 717). Ordinary people who uphold and propagate the Mystic Law are themselves Buddhas; this is the essence of the Daishonin's Buddhism.

The state of Buddhahood manifests in our every action; the wisdom and compassion of the Buddha manifest in our lives from moment to moment. Truly, this is the meaning of "each life-moment in the phantom city is a life-moment in the treasure land."

Saito: Also, great importance attaches to the Daishonin's statement, "'identical to' indicates Nam-myoho-renge-kyo." He is saying that Nam-myoho-renge-kyo is the driving force for manifesting the life-moment of Buddhahood amid the reality of the nine worlds.

Endo: Regarding the principle of the oneness of the phantom city with the treasure land, I recall that you, President Ikeda, have said that kosen-rufu is like the flow of a great river. We tend to have an image of kosen-rufu as a kind of goal that is reached when a great many people embrace the Mystic Law. But you went beyond that perspective, explaining that the practice of spreading Buddhism is itself kosen-rufu.

The principle of the unity of phantom city and the treasure land reminds me of the words of Goethe that you borrowed to express your feeling when you took faith after meeting President Toda: "It is not enough to take steps which may some day lead to a goal; each step must be itself a goal and a step likewise."[11]

Ikeda: To view kosen-rufu as a point when an ideal has been attained is not without meaning. But I wanted to emphasize the importance of the spirit to spread Buddhism. We must not think of the "journey," the process of achieving this ideal, as just a means. Those who make this mistake, using others as mere tools to achieve some end, may repeat the mistakes of revolutionary movements of the past that produced innumerable tragedies.

Buddhism is a religion that exists for the sake of human beings. Under no circumstances should people be victimized or turned into a means to an end. That is my conviction as a Buddhist.

To advance, we have to set up "phantom cities" in the form of targets. But on a deeper level, efforts to proceed toward and reach these "phantom cities" are themselves the actions of the Buddha. And the arena for these endeavors is itself the "treasure land."

Saito: Attaining Buddhahood is not like reaching the goal in a board game. To view it as representing a final destination or point of attainment is, ultimately, an expedient means. As long as there is life, there is motion and change; therefore, there's no such thing as a static final destination. Our actions in continuing to struggle for kosen-rufu are themselves the actions of the Buddha.

Ikeda: It is important, therefore, that we thoroughly enjoy all of our activities. Who has ever heard of a Buddha whose life is filled with suffering? Developing the state of life to delight in working hard for kosen-rufu, to view challenging circumstances as opportunities to create even more good fortune and to further expand our state of life prove that the world of Buddhahood is shining in our lives.

Endo: Those whose attitude is to complain when a new target appears cannot actualize the principle of the phantom city is identical to the treasure land in their lives.

Ikeda: It wouldn't be so bad, perhaps, if people could develop a state of life in which they could really enjoy complaining!

As long as we are alive, we will have problems of one kind or another. That's only natural. But it's ridiculous to be constantly reeling back and forth between feelings of elation and dejection every time something comes up.

We need to earnestly and steadfastly challenge ourselves to achieve goals. Resolving to overcome all obstacles, we must open a path forward. When we look back later, we will see that these moments, while perhaps trying, were in fact the most fulfilling and rewarding times of our lives. They will be a treasury of golden memories, great scenes in the eternal drama of our lives throughout the past, present and future.

Nichiren Daishonin says: "Now, when Nichiren and his followers chant Nam-myoho-renge-kyo, they are asserting that the phantom city is identical to the treasure land. These mountains, valleys and broad plains where we live are all, every one of them, the treasure land of Eternally Tranquil Light" (GZ, 734).

This explains the state of life of us who embrace and practice the Mystic Law. Wherever we may be, and no matter what our circumstances, in the depths of our lives we can experience the "greatest of all joys" (GZ, 788).

NOTES

1. Soren Kierkegaard, *The Present Age*, trans. Alesander Dru and Walter Lowrie (London: Oxford University Press, 1940), p. 3.

2. From the translator's commentary to the Japanese edition: Soren Kierkegaard, *Gendai no Hihan* (The Present Age), trans. Keisaburo Masuda (Tokyo: Iwanami Shoten, 1985), pp. 219–20.

3. Soren Kierkegaard, *Die Tagebücher* (Diaries) (Dusseldorf/Cologne: Eugen Diederichs Verlag, 1963), vol. 2, p. 98.

4. Ibid., p. 31.

5. The earliest Chinese translation of the Saddharamapundarika-sutra (Lotus Sutra), consisting of twenty-seven chapters in ten volumes. This translation (dated 286) corresponds with the Myoho-renge-kyo (406) of Kumarajiva in most respects, except that it contains several parables that the latter omits.

6. An extremely long period of time deriving from ancient Indian tradition. The length of a *kalpa* is described in various ways. According to one method of reckoning, a medium *kalpa* would equal nearly sixteen million years.

7. From *Words and Phrases of the Lotus Sutra*.

8. *Toda Josei Zenshu* (Collected Works of Josei Toda), vol. 3, p. 73.

9. Josei Toda, *Wakaki hi no shuki — Gokuchuki* (Notes From My Youth: Prison Record) (Tokyo: Seiga Shobo, 1971), pp. 180–81.

10. *Toda Josei Zenshu*, vol. 1, p. 304.

11. Johann Eckermann, *Words of Goethe* (New York: Tudor Publishing, 1949), p. 18.

PART SIX

"Prophecy of Enlightenment for Five Hundred Disciples" and "Prophecies Conferred On Learners and Adepts" Chapters

6 The Voice-hearers Awaken

Saito: President Ikeda, you once met with Dr. Margarita I. Voroby-ova-Desyatovskaya of the Institute of Oriental Studies, Russian Academy of Sciences, who has done a great deal of research on the Lotus Sutra. I found the discussion profoundly moving.

Dr. Vorobyova-Desyatovskaya lost her husband at a young age and raised their son alone. Undeterred, for four decades she has tirelessly pursued her research on the sutra. Adding to the challenge, for most of that time her country was governed by a totalitarian regime. Her study of Buddhism cannot by any stretch of the imagination have been easy.

Your discussion affirmed the universality of the Lotus Sutra, which has transcended national boundaries to capture the hearts of truly enormous numbers of people living under widely varying circumstances.

Ikeda: Dr. Vorobyova-Desyatovskaya is a person of character. She possesses genuine humility and profound humanity. Perhaps it is for this reason that she has grasped the outstanding merits of the Lotus Sutra. I could see that she has a deep understanding of the sutra.

How can one grasp the essence of the paean to humankind that pulses in the Lotus Sutra? The truth of the Lotus Sutra can be found only within the human heart; it definitely cannot be comprehended with the intellect alone. Therein lies the fascination of studying the Lotus Sutra and also the difficulty. Dr. Voroby-ova-Desyatovskaya's research on the Lotus Sutra touches on this essence, on the human heart.

Suda: Her answer to why the Lotus Sutra has been embraced by so many people and spread so widely was very clear. She explained it has engendered a completely new way of thinking. She characterized this as the understanding that people are fundamentally free and can themselves change the course of their destiny. This perspective of the Lotus Sutra inwardly liberates people; and this, she said, has held such a powerful attraction.

Endo: Dr. Vorobyova-Desyatovskaya's remarks on the important role that the Lotus Sutra may play in the twenty-first century also impressed me.

The Lotus Sutra, she said, prompts each person to reflect on the purpose for his or her actions and ultimate goals in life as well as the direction in which the human race is heading. She suggested that the Lotus Sutra's function is to get people to think along these lines.

Saito: Dr. Vorobyova-Desyatovskaya at one point credited you, President Ikeda, and the SGI with breathing new life into her research. She also said that she hoped her work would be of service to humankind. Hearing these words, pervaded with her sense of mission to dedicate herself to the good of others, was most refreshing.

Ikeda: To work for the sake of others—that is the spirit of a true scholar. Whatever the field, without this spirit one cannot accomplish anything great. In the present age, this spirit seems to have been forgotten.

Suda: There are even some who feel that other people's happiness is their misfortune, and that other people's misfortunes are a cause for their happiness.

Saito: Such people are sad victims of the competitive society we live in, their lives rendered dark and perverse.

Ikeda: The truth is that devoting ourselves to others' happiness is a necessary condition for becoming genuinely happy ourselves.

Endo: From studies in psychology, Carl Jung and other psychologists have described the ideal life as something like this: In infancy, to have a sense of security in being embraced in the love of parents and others; during youth, to make tenacious efforts to seek something higher, something sacred or divine; in middle age, to serve others; and in old age, to live with hope, wisdom and a sense of absolute confidence in the value of the life that one has led.

Ikeda: Working tenaciously to seek something lofty, serving others, and leading a long and fulfilled existence—this is very similar to the way of life of a bodhisattva. Restoring such a way of life will be a fundamental concern of the twenty-first century.

THE STRUGGLES OF THE CITIZENS OF LENINGRAD

Suda: The siege of Leningrad (present-day St. Petersburg), which came up in your discussion with Dr. Vorobyova-Desyatovskaya, produced many instances of human drama, of people acting with the spirit of bodhisattvas.

Ikeda: As many as a million citizens are said to have perished when the Nazis blockaded the city for almost nine hundred days. The majority died of starvation.

A poet put her deceased husband on a child's sled and pulled it to Piskarevsky Cemetery on the city's outskirts. It was painful for her to place her husband's body along with the many other corpses piled there. As she walked along the road, exhausted and hungry, having to stop frequently to rest, she would pass women pulling sleds bearing corpses similarly wrapped in sheets or blankets. She wrote: "Really will there be a victory for me? What comfort will I find in it? Let me be. Let me be forgotten. I will live alone. . . ."[1]

I once laid a wreath of flowers and offered heartfelt prayers for the eternal happiness of those buried in Piskarevsky Cemetery. One headstone bears the inscription, "Let no one forget; let nothing be forgotten!"[2]

The history of Leningrad calls out to us with the weight of a million lives, each unique and irreplaceable: "Peace! Realize peace, no matter what it takes!" "Such a tragedy must never again be repeated!" To bring this unvoiced cry to all people, I will continue to travel the world, meet with people and conduct dialogue.

Saito: What sustained the citizens of Leningrad amid such hardship?

Ikeda: Various explanations have been given, but radio broadcasts seem to have been an important factor.

Endo: All transmissions were by wired radio. Possession of ordinary radio receivers was reportedly made a capital offense [at the outset of the war, the aim being to prevent citizens from listening to foreign broadcasts].

Ikeda: That's right. Without food and holed up in cold rooms with nothing to do, people looked forward to the poetry readings and musical performances that came to them over the radio.

But if just staying alive was an ordeal for those listening, those making the transmissions were also hanging on for dear life. There was a poet who, after finishing a reading for a broadcast, collapsed in the studio from hunger and died several days later. In another instance, a singer who performed was so frail he had to support himself with a cane. He died that very night.

In the studio, there was a rake-like wooden device in the shape of the letter T. This was to support performers if they were too weak to stand. The director of the studio encouraged the performers with all his being: "In thousands of apartments they are awaiting your voice."[3]

When the radio transmissions were discontinued because of a power shortage, citizens eagerly offered to have their power rations cut so that transmissions could resume.[4]

The desperate spirit of those involved in the broadcasts to give hope and inspiration ignited the flame of courage in the people's frozen hearts. Despite interruptions in the supply of food, heat and light, and when hope itself had been lost, it was the voices and words calling out to their spirits that sustained people's lives. Not only the stomach grows hungry; the spirit, too, requires nourishment.

Saito: This really makes me contemplate just how important culture is.

Ikeda: It is said that thousands of sailors in the Russian navy while at sea read Dostoevsky and Tolstoy.[5] Some writers in Leningrad got the idea to preserve the experience of life under siege in a book. But the authorities would not give them permission. By the time approval finally came through, many of the writers had died, and those who survived were too weak and emaciated to work. Ultimately, the project came to naught. Journalist Harrison Salisbury describes the situation: "People held themselves together by the consciousness of being needed. They began to die when they had nothing to do. Nothing-to-do was more terrible than a bombing raid."[6]

The reason for the delay in permission was that no one among the authorities wanted to take responsibility for approving the project. Bureaucratism robbed the writers of their hope and with it their lives. It's a fearful thing when those in positions of authority do not understand the people's hearts. This is a point that leaders in the SGI need to grasp from the depth of their being.

At any rate, it was the spirit and determination to hang on for others, to sing for the sake of all, and to write for the sake of posterity that sustained these individuals and enabled them to support one another. Our true selves shine and the underlying strength of our lives wells forth when we exert ourselves for others. This is human nature. And this is the way of life the Lotus Sutra teaches.

In this chapter, we'll discuss "Prophecy of Enlightenment for Five Hundred Disciples" and "Prophecies Conferred on Learners and Adepts,"[7] the eighth and ninth chapters of the Lotus Sutra. These chapters conclude the teaching of the replacement of the three vehicles of the voice-hearers, *pratyekabuddhas* and bodhisattvas (Learning, Realization and Bodhisattva) with the one vehicle of Buddhahood, which is the main theme of the Lotus Sutra's first half (or theoretical teaching).

FROM "PEOPLE WHO ARE SAVED" TO "PEOPLE WHO SAVE OTHERS"

The way followed by the sons of the Buddha,
because they are well learned in expedient means,
is wonderful beyond conception.
They know how most beings delight in a little Law
and are fearful of great wisdom.
Therefore the bodhisattvas
pose as voice-hearers or pratyekabuddhas,
employing countless expedient means
to convert the diVerent kinds of living beings.
They proclaim themselves to be voice-hearers
and say they are far removed from the Buddha way,
and so bring emancipation to immeasurable multitudes,
allowing them all to achieve success.
Limited in aspiration, lazy and indolent though the
multitudes are,
Bit by bit they are led to the attainment of
Buddhahood.

> Inwardly, in secret, the sons act as bodhisattvas,
> but outwardly they show themselves as voice-hearers.
> They seem to be lessening desires out of hatred for birth
>   and death,
> but in truth they are purifying the Buddha lands.
> Before the multitude they seem possessed of the three
>   poisons
> or manifest the signs of heretical views.
> My disciples in this manner
> use expedient means to save living beings.
> (LS8, 146–47)

Saito: As is clear from the titles, the main theme of these two chapters is the bestowal of prophecy. They contain the culmination of the Buddha's predictions of enlightenment for the voice-hearers.

The Great Teacher T'ien-t'ai of China designates the eight chapters from "Expedient Means," the second chapter, through "Learners and Adepts," the ninth chapter, as the "revelation" section of the theoretical teaching. From a doctrinal standpoint, these eight chapters explain the replacement of the three vehicles with the one vehicle. In terms of narrative drama, however, the central element is probably the bestowal of prophecies of enlightenment upon the voice-hearers.

Ikeda: It is the drama of the voice-hearers opening their eyes. Without understanding the significance of this drama, one cannot grasp the true meaning of the doctrine of the replacement of the three vehicles with the one vehicle.

What is the awakening of the voice-hearers? In conclusion, it has to do with their changing from people who are saved to people who save others. They awaken, in other words, to the great vow to unfailingly lead others to happiness.

The voice-hearers had sought the Buddha's teaching out of the desire to escape—to be "saved" from—the sufferings of this impure world. The Buddha, understanding their minds, first expounded the Hinayana teachings as a way for them to gain release from suffering.

Endo: Their mistake lay in becoming attached to these teachings.

Suda: In the fourth chapter, "Belief and Understanding," the voice-hearers confess, "in the midst of birth and death we undergo burning anxieties, delusions, and ignorance, delighting in and clinging to lesser doctrines" (LS4, 86).

Ikeda: "Lesser doctrines" means the Hinayana teachings. But the Buddha's true intention is not contained in the Hinayana. The Buddha did not want his disciples to wind up merely seeking to be led to salvation, and so he expounded the Lotus Sutra, which clarifies his true intention.

What you should seek, he tells the voice-hearers, is not the enlightenment of the Hinayana but the wisdom of the Buddha. He is saying in effect: "I want to enable all people to gain the Buddha's wisdom and raise their state of life so that they can freely lead others to happiness just as the Buddha does." This is the Buddha's true intention.

Saito: The expression "just as the Buddha does" points to the oneness of mentor and disciple.

Ikeda: Exactly. Those who hear the Lotus Sutra and cherish the same wish as their mentor—"I want to save people just as the Buddha does" are bodhisattvas of the Lotus Sutra. This wish or vow is at the same time the "awareness of the Buddha's children"—the realization: "I am a child of the Buddha, and therefore I can inherit in its entirety the wisdom that is the Buddha's legacy."

A little earlier, we talked about the bodhisattva-like activities of the people responsible for radio transmissions during the siege of Leningrad. It can also be said that Shakyamuni's voice-hearer disciples change from being merely voice-hearers who hear the Buddha's voice into voice-hearers who, as bodhisattvas, enable others to hear the Buddha's voice.

The eight chapters that make up the revelation section of the theoretical teaching depict the drama of the voice-hearers carrying out their human revolution along precisely these lines. The chapters we have discussed up to this point show Shariputra and the four great voice-hearer disciples enacting this drama of awakening. But in "Five Hundred Disciples" and "Learners and Adepts," we finally see all of the voice-hearers becoming involved.

THE PREDICTION OF ENLIGHTENMENT

Suda: Let us start by discussing the general flow of these two chapters. At the outset of "Five Hundred Disciples," Shakyamuni bestows a prophecy of enlightenment on Purna, who had delighted upon hearing the Buddha preach in "The Parable of the Phantom City," the seventh chapter. Among Shakyamuni's disciples, Purna was known as foremost in preaching the Law and also in eloquence.

Endo: At one time, Purna wished to spread Shakyamuni's teaching among the people in another land. A Buddhist text records an episode prior to his departure. Some have argued that it is actually about a different person with the same name. Still, I would like to share it because, scholarly disagreements notwithstanding, it sheds light on Purna's character as the disciple foremost in preaching the Law.

When Purna tells the Buddha he is about to embark on a journey of propagation, Shakyamuni says to him: "Purna, the people of that land are known to be rough-tempered. Without understanding the reason of things, they constantly speak ill of others. They will very likely deride and abuse you. When that happens, what will you do?"

Purna replies, "If that is the case, I will say to myself, 'Because they do not strike me with their fists, the inhabitants of this land are good people.'"

"Then what will you do," the Buddha continued, "if they strike you?"

"I will say to myself," said Purna, "'Because they do not beat me with staves, the inhabitants of this country are good people.'"

"If they beat you with staves, what will you do?"

"I will say to myself, 'Because they do not lash me with whips, they are good people.'"

"What if they lash you with whips?"

"I will say to myself, 'Because they do not injure me with swords, they are good people.'"

"What if they injure you with swords?"

"I will say to myself, 'Because they do not kill me, they are good people.'"

"What, then, will you do, Purna, if you are killed by the people of that country?"

The disciple answered without hesitation: "There are some who seek death. Because in being killed I would, without seeking death, be discarding this poor, impure body for the sake of the Buddhist Law, it would bring me the greatest joy."

Shakyamuni's mind was put at ease. "Very well, then, Purna," he said. "If you have such determination, you will be all right. Go then." [8]

Purna, it is related, went to that land and converted many people to the Buddha's teaching.

Ikeda: He realized his wish. Purna's name is variously translated into Chinese as "Wishes Fulfilled" and "Fulfillment." True to his name, I'm sure his life was indeed one of great fulfillment.

Suda: Because he was known as foremost in preaching the Law and foremost in eloquence, we can see him as someone skilled at discourse, who possessed a refreshing eloquence. The Sanskrit text of "Five Hundred Disciples" says, "Purna reveals the Law to the four kinds of believers, teaches them, praises and encourages them, and causes them to feel delight, and he never tires of expounding the Law." As this suggests, what he possessed was more than superficial technique, he was more than just a skillful conversationalist.

Ikeda: Kumarajiva's translation of the sutra speaks of Purna's "ability in teaching, benefiting and delighting the four kinds of believers" (LS8, 144). He caused people to feel joy by preaching the Law to them. That is where Purna placed his emphasis. When we truly feel delight from the bottom of our hearts, those around us change.

What was the source of Purna's eloquence? One factor was probably his passion for spreading and sharing with others the teaching of his mentor. No matter how skilled at speaking people may be, if they lack burning passion, they cannot move others' hearts. And the source of passion is conviction. Also, I think it was Purna's honesty and integrity. He was a person of sincerity. No doubt many were touched by his warmheartedness and thoughtfulness.

Saito: In "Five Hundred Disciples," Purna receives a specific prophecy that in the future he will become a Buddha called Law Bright Thus Come One. I think this means that he will illuminate people's lives with the brilliant light of the Law.

Ikeda: SGI members who exert themselves for kosen-rufu similarly illuminate the lives of many others.

Endo: When they hear the specific prophecy for Purna, the twelve hundred *arhats* rejoice. Shakyamuni says he will bestow prophecies on them, too, and predicts enlightenment for five hundred. This is where "five hundred disciples" in the chapter's title comes from. These five hundred are represented by Kaundinya, who was Shakyamuni's very first disciple.

Arhats are voice-hearers of the highest rank who have attained the enlightenment of the Hinayana teachings. It may be that the five hundred *arhats* were disciples who played a central role in the Buddhist order from its early days. In other texts, there are accounts of Shakyamuni taking five hundred disciples with him on journeys to preach the Law. This may also be why, in his prophecy of enlightenment for them, Shakyamuni gives all five hundred the same name — Universal Brightness Thus Come One.

As for the remaining seven hundred disciples, no specific prophecy of enlightenment is made for them in the sutra. At the outset of "The Teacher of the Law" chapter, however, Shakyamuni predicts enlightenment for all those in the assembly where the Lotus Sutra is being expounded. We may surmise that these seven hundred disciples are among the recipients of that prophecy.

Suda: At the beginning of "Learners and Adepts," prophecies of enlightenment are bestowed first on Ananda and Rahula. Among Shakyamuni's disciples, Ananda was said to be foremost in hearing the Buddha's teachings — that is, he listened to Shakyamuni expound the Law more than any other disciple — and after Shakyamuni's death he played a key role in efforts to compile his teachings as sutras. Rahula was Shakyamuni's son from before he had renounced the world. Among the Buddha's disciples, he was known as foremost in inconspicuous practice.

Shakyamuni also makes predictions of enlightenment for two thousand learners and adepts. These are voice-hearers who have not yet reached the stage of *arhat*. A learner means someone still engaged in the process of learning; an adept is someone whose studies are complete.

Ikeda: It is interesting to note that the original term for "adept" is composed of two characters meaning "no learning," the implication being that the person has completed his or her learning and has no further need of study. In modern Japanese usage, this term has exactly the opposite meaning — that of "lack of learning," "uneducated" or "ignorant." At first glance, therefore, unaware of this distinction, it would seem to suggest that the ignorant are above those with learning!

Suda: Yet, despite the distinction between learners and adepts, they are all voice-hearers who have not yet attained the enlightenment of *arhats*.

Saito: In short, in these two chapters, prophecies of enlightenment are bestowed on all voice-hearers irrespective of their degree of attainment in practice. The specific predictions of the titles of the Buddhas they will become and the names of the *kalpas* when and the lands where they will be active are as follows.

Shakyamuni predicts that Purna, in an age called Treasure Bright and a land called Good and Pure, will become a Buddha named Law Bright Thus Come One. He predicts that the five hundred *arhats* will become Buddhas called Universal Brightness Thus Come One. He predicts that Ananda, in an age called Wonderful Sound Filling Everywhere and a land called Ever-Standing Victory Banner, will become a Buddha called Mountain Sea Wisdom Unrestricted Power King Thus Come One. Rahula, he predicts, will become a Buddha called Stepping on Seven Treasure Flowers Thus Come One. And he predicts that the two thousand learners and adepts will become Buddhas called Jewel Sign Thus Come One.

Later, in "Encouraging Devotion," Shakyamuni says, "I earlier made a general statement saying that all the voice-hearers had received such a prophecy" (LS13, 191).

Ikeda: As I have mentioned before, the bestowal of prophecy upon the voice-hearers means a bestowal of prophecy upon all people. The promise of enlightenment does not apply only to the voice-hearers; all people can attain Buddhahood. All people can inherit the Buddha's wisdom and become capable of leading others to happiness. This idea is indicated in the prophecy of enlightenment for all voice-hearers, in which no distinction is made among *arhats*, learners and adepts.

Nichiren Daishonin says, "T'ien-t'ai established that the attainment of Buddhahood by persons of the two vehicles is proof that all living beings without exception can become Buddhas" (WND, 58). In the provisional teachings that preceded the Lotus Sutra, all voice-hearers were deemed to be incapable of ever attaining Buddhahood. But in the Lotus Sutra, they are revealed to be capable of attaining Buddhahood. This clarifies that not only the people of the two vehicles but all beings in the Ten Worlds can attain Buddhahood.

That is because the life of one voice-hearer is endowed with all Ten Worlds. So the bestowal of a prophecy of enlightenment upon one voice-hearer indicates that all Ten Worlds of life can manifest the world of Buddhahood. And the fact that the Ten Worlds can manifest the world of Buddhahood means that living beings in any world can attain Buddhahood.

On the other hand, if the voice-hearers—those in the world of Learning—could not become Buddhas, it would mean that the world of Learning in the lives of bodhisattvas, as well as the world of Learning in the life of the Buddha, could not manifest the world of Buddhahood.

Endo: If neither bodhisattvas nor Buddhas could attain Buddhahood, Buddhism would not exist.

Ikeda: The enlightenment of the voice-hearers and *pratyekabuddhas* (the people of the two vehicles), therefore, is the very cornerstone of Buddhism.

Now, the voice-hearers comprised people who were closest to Shakyamuni, people constantly at the Buddha's side. If Shakyamuni could not enable them to attain Buddhahood, then we would have to wonder about the purpose of Buddhism.

The voice-hearers and *pratyekabuddhas* were held to have "scorched the seeds" of Buddhahood in their lives. That

Shakyamuni's enables them to become Buddhas reveals the power of the Lotus Sutra to enable all people to attain Buddhahood. The sutra in effect proclaims to all people: "You, too, can develop the same state of life as the Buddha." This is the spirit of the bestowal of prophecy.

Suda: Nichiren Daishonin expresses the same spirit with his own words. In the "Record of the Orally Transmitted Teachings," it says: "Now, when Nichiren and his followers chant Nam-myoho-renge-kyo, they are bestowing on both learners and adepts a prophecy that, as Shakyamuni Buddha said, 'all persons [will be] equal to me, without any distinction between us,' are they not?... On all of them, wise and ignorant alike, we bestow the prophecy of Nam-myoho-renge-kyo, 'forcing them to listen, though it angers them'" (GZ, 735).

Ikeda: That is the spirit of kosen-rufu—to expound the Mystic Law to people whether they are wise or ignorant, whether they believe or disbelieve. Those who reject the teaching will be led to enlightenment through a "poison-drum" relationship, that is, through the benefit of a reverse relationship. This is the true bestowal of prophecy. SGI members have put this teaching into practice. The spirit of the Lotus Sutra is alive and well within the SGI.

THE "UNIFICATION OF THE PRACTITIONERS" AND "UNIFICATION OF THE TEACHINGS"

Saito: As we have discussed previously, starting in "Simile and Parable," one after another the voice-hearers, beginning with Shariputra, receive predictions of future enlightenment. This signifies their transformation from people who are saved into people who save others. The voice-hearers, in other words, become bodhisattvas.

Endo: In "Expedient Means," Shakyamuni says, "I employ only the single vehicle way / to teach and convert the bodhisattvas, / I have no voice-hearer disciples" (LS2, 45). This is the "unification of the practitioners" (i.e., the unification of the persons practicing the three vehicles within the one vehicle); and we should note that it is confirmed already in "Expedient Means." This means that all who are instructed through the path of the one vehicle (i.e., the Lotus Sutra) are bodhisattvas.

Saito: Unification means amalgamating things usually thought of as distinct or separate by viewing them from a higher perspective. In terms of the teaching, unification means that the Buddha expounds only the one Buddha vehicle and that there are no separate teachings of the three vehicles (of voice-hearers, *pratyekabuddhas* and bodhisattvas). When we view the three vehicles as distinct teachings, we view them from the standpoint of the people who receive these teachings. From the Buddha's perspective, they are unified; he is expounding only one path to attaining Buddhahood, and that is the one Buddha vehicle.

In terms of the practitioners, the Buddha teaches only bodhisattvas who cherish the aspiration to attain Buddhahood; there are no distinctions of voice-hearer, *pratyekabuddha* and bodhisattva among the disciples whom he instructs. From the standpoint of the "unification of the practitioners," the Buddha discerns that all people in the depths of their lives aspire to become Buddhas and have a seeking spirit for the Buddha's wisdom. From that perspective, all people alike are unified as bodhisattvas.

At the outset of "Five Hundred Disciples," Purna, having in the preceding chapter, "Phantom City," heard Shakyamuni expound the causes and conditions uniting the disciples with the mentor since the remote past of major world system dust particle *kalpas*, realizes "the wish that we have had deep in our hearts from the start" (LS8, 144). In other words, he indicates that, since the distant past, he has yearned to attain Buddhahood and has carried out bodhisattva practice together with his mentor, Shakyamuni. Before becoming a voice-hearer, he was a bodhisattva; and this, he realizes, is his true identity.

The unification of the practitioners of the Lotus Sutra clarifies that deep in their hearts all people are originally bodhisattvas. From this perspective, all people are equal, not in terms of appearance or abilities but on the level of life itself; they are a single unified entity.

Ikeda: This most egalitarian understanding of life is substantiated by the principles of the 'mutual possession of the Ten Worlds' and 'three thousand realms in a single moment of life.'

Suda: In "Learners and Adepts," it is clarified that Ananda is foremost in hearing the Buddha's teachings, not in his practice as a voice-hearer but based on his original wish as a bodhisattva. This is because, through hearing the Law continuously as the Buddha's attendant and relaying it to others, he can guide others to attain Buddhahood.

Endo: The same is true of Rahula's virtue of being foremost in inconspicuous practice. Rahula was born as the son of Shakyamuni. In becoming Shakyamuni's disciple after the latter attained enlightenment, it is explained, Rahula did not become a voice-hearer but carried out inconspicuous practice with the single-minded hope of attaining Buddhahood. His practice, of which others were unaware (hence, called "inconspicuous"), was bodhisattva practice. The same is true of the voice-hearers at the levels of learner and adept.

Ikeda: And so the "Five Hundred Disciples" and "Learners and Adepts" chapters reveal that all voice-hearers are originally bodhisattvas. We can view the revelation of the true identity of the voice-hearers as the theme of these two chapters.

Of course, from a more profound perspective, even the view

that they are originally bodhisattvas or that they have secured their attainment of Buddhahood is from the standpoint of the theoretical teaching, or the Lotus Sutra's first half. From the standpoint of the essential teaching, or the latter half of the sutra (i.e., in terms of the implicit meaning), it is the revelation that "our minds are originally that of a Buddha" (GZ, 788).

In the theoretical teaching, a person carries out bodhisattva practice and then becomes a Buddha; in other words, one proceeds from the cause to the effect, from the nine worlds to the world of Buddhahood. In contrast, the essential teaching takes the position that a Buddha enlightened from the remote past carries out bodhisattva practice; in other words, one proceeds from the effect to the cause, from the world of Buddhahood to the nine worlds. From this standpoint, the life of a bodhisattva is in fact none other than the life of the Buddha.

Also, their "wish that we have had deep in our hearts from the start" means that they base themselves on their awareness of the Buddha's having sown the seed of enlightenment in their lives in the remote past.

To put it another way, as they earnestly made efforts to become Buddhas, the voice-hearers were proceeding from cause to effect (i.e., practicing from the standpoint of theoretical teaching). But once they ascend the mountain of the Lotus Sutra and look around, the world at once opens up and they behold the vast panorama of the universe. At that point, they understand that the Buddha enlightened since the remote past has been ceaselessly carrying out bodhisattva practice to guide the beings of the Ten Worlds. (This is the standpoint of the essential teaching, of proceeding from the effect to the cause.) This Buddha carries out this activity, without interruption or change, eternally—over past, present and future.

When the voice-hearers look at themselves, they realize that, as ordinary people from time without beginning, they have always been one with the Buddha. At one with the mentor, they are carrying out bodhisattva practice toward the goal of kosen-rufu. The essential teaching reveals to the beings in the assembly this profound aspect of their lives.

RECAPTURE YOUR HUMANITY

Ikeda: Broadly speaking, the unification of the practitioners means transcending all differences among people by viewing things from a deeper level and perceiving that all are equally worthy of respect.

During the Cold War, for example, the doors of the communist world were closed tight, as though frozen over with ice or barred by iron. But there was no reason why, differences between capitalism and socialism notwithstanding, exchange could not take place based on the recognition of a common humanity. That was my conviction.

Saito: When you went to the former Soviet Union, many people criticized you, asking, for example, why a religious leader was traveling to an atheist nation. But your reply was clear: "People are there." I recall being moved by your actions, thinking that this was truly an example of the unification of the practitioners in the present age.

Endo: In concrete terms, exchange on a human level means exchange in the realms of culture and education. To cultivate such exchange is truly to carry out the practice of the Lotus Sutra.

Ikeda: Russia has produced many great writers, including Tolstoy and Dostoevsky, who urged people to transcend differences among themselves and return to the human being.

Suda: Dostoevsky, like Dr. Vorobyova-Desyatovskaya, was born in what is today St. Petersburg.

Ikeda: That's right. In the late nineteenth century, Russian intellectuals were divided into two camps: "Westernists," who were enamored with the thought and tradition of Western Europe, and nationalistic "Slavophiles." Dostoevsky characterized the members of both of these groups as "unhappy wanderers" who had become alienated from the people. He cried: "Oh, all this Slavophilism and this Westernism is a great, although historically inevitable, misunderstanding.... Yes, the Russian's destiny is incontestably all-European and universal. To become a genuine and all-round Russian means, perhaps (and this you should remember), to become brother of all men." [9]

"Become a human being!" he cried, in other words. "By doing so, you will become the friend of all people."

Endo: I am reminded of your impressions on visiting the State Hermitage Museum in Leningrad. You wrote: "In the distant future, after countless generations of our grandchildren's grandchildren, when people sift through the past, they will be struck only by the brilliance of human life itself, which far transcends the realm of social systems such as socialism and capitalism. That brilliance is the source of all humanistic and creative culture." [10]

That was more than twenty years ago. Humanity, it seems, is approaching this realization.

Ikeda: Russia is a great country. It has produced some of the world's finest literature and music. And, having concluded its grandiose experiment with socialism, it is now struggling to open a new phase in human history.

The people of Russia are pioneers of humankind. It seems to me they are taking the lead in dealing with problems that the rest of humanity will have to face in the future. Therefore, their worries are great, and their mission is likewise immense.

Dostoevsky writes of "becoming brother of all men." What a wonderful sense of mission this is! We have a great deal still to learn from the lofty spirit of Russia.

Incidentally, in connection with the "Five Hundred Disciples" chapter, we cannot omit discussion of the parable of the gem in the robe.

The Parable of the Gem in the Robe

Endo: Yes. After receiving a prophecy of enlightenment from Shakyamuni, the five hundred disciples relate the parable of the gem in the robe as "evidence" of their joy.

Forgetting themselves in their elation, the five hundred *arhats* kneel down in veneration at Shakyamuni's feet. They regret their mistake in having been satisfied with the small wisdom of *arhats* and not seeking the wisdom of the Thus Come One and reproach themselves. Describing themselves in their earlier foolishness as having been like a poor wanderer, they relate the parable of the gem in the robe. It goes as follows.[11]

A poor man visits the house of a dear friend. There he feasts and drinks heartily and falls asleep in a drunken stupor. At that time, the friend suddenly has to go off on urgent official business. Before leaving, the friend sews a priceless jewel into the lining of the man's robe. Because the poor man is asleep drunk, he is completely unaware of this. And he remains ignorant of the jewel later as he goes wandering from one country to another. Over the years, he becomes completely destitute and his life is filled with suffering. He works to clothe and feed himself, but his suffering continues. And whenever he gets a little money, he feels fully content.

Ikeda: Many people today are, spiritually, in similarly precarious positions.

Suda: At length, the friend encounters the man again. Seeing his ragged appearance, he tells him: "Why should you have to do all this for the sake of food and clothing? In the past I wanted to make certain you would be able to live in ease...and so...I took a priceless jewel and sewed it in the lining of your robe. It must still be there now. But you did not know about it, and fretted and wore yourself out trying to provide a living for yourself" (LS8, 151).

The poor man then sees the gem of which his friend has told him and greatly rejoices.

Saito: What is the "priceless jewel"? The sutra describes it as the "determination to seek comprehensive wisdom" and the "desire for comprehensive wisdom" (LS8, 151). "Comprehensive wisdom" is the wisdom of the Buddha. In other words, the priceless jewel is the spirit to seek the Buddha's wisdom, the spirit of yearning to attain Buddhahood.

As explained in the "Phantom City" chapter, this determination was formed in the lives of the Buddha's disciples during the remote past of major world system dust particle *kalpas* when they heard the Lotus Sutra from Shakyamuni, who was then a bodhisattva. In the parable, this is represented by the gem that had been sewn into the lining of the man's robe by his good friend. The good friend, needless to say, is Shakyamuni.

Endo: The man's wandering in poverty and his contentment with his precarious existence represents the state of life of the voice-hearers, who had studied the Hinayana teachings, felt satisfied with the enlightenment of *arhats* and did not seek the wisdom of the Buddha.

The man's re-encounter with the good friend and finding out about the priceless jewel corresponds to the voice-hearers now hearing the Lotus Sutra. That is, through hearing the Lotus Sutra in the present, they recall the "original wish" to attain Buddhahood they had conceived in the remote past.

Ikeda: They return to their "true selves." This is the "awakening of the voice-hearers." They wake up from the drunken stupor of darkness (that is, ignorance about the true nature of their lives).

A key word, here, is *return.* They perceive the Law that is the wellspring of their own lives. It is a matter of "returning to the self." It was the stupor of darkness that had caused them to forget this. T'ien-t'ai says that this stupor may be either heavy or light.[12]

Saito: There is heavy drunkenness and light drunkenness. Heavy drunkenness is the state where one completely has no recollection. This is comparable to being dead drunk. Light drunkenness is like the state of someone who is only slightly inebriated at the time but who afterwards forgets everything.

Ikeda: While there are differences in degree of drunkenness, in either case the person fails to remember. That is what darkness means. Because their hearts are shrouded in darkness, they cannot understand the wonder of their own lives.

Suda: People who are drunk have a hard time accepting they are drunk.

Saito: Also, trying to wake someone who has passed out from drink is next to impossible.

Ikeda: It seems that for most of us it's only after receiving a lot of strict encouragement from our seniors in Buddhist practice that we finally wake up in faith.

Suda: In the "Orally Transmitted Teachings," the Daishonin says, "Now, when Nichiren and his followers chant Nam-myoho-renge-kyo, they are in effect sobering up from the wine of ignorance" (GZ, 735). The sense of exhilaration we feel when chanting daimoku is the joy of awakening from the stupor of darkness.

Endo: The sutra says, "When the poor man saw the jewel / his heart was filled with great joy" (LS8, 152). The "Orally Transmitted Teachings" states: "This passage refers to the great joy we experience when we understand for the first time that our life has from the beginning been a Buddha. Nam-myoho-renge-kyo is the greatest of all joys" (GZ, 788).

Ikeda: We each have "from the beginning been a Buddha." The "Five Hundred Disciples" chapter speaks of the "wish that we [the Buddha's disciples] have had deep in our hearts from the start." In a nutshell, this is the great wish to lead all people to enlightenment. It is this great wish that the voice-hearers have recollected.

Nichiren Daishonin says, "'Great wish' refers to the propagation of the Lotus Sutra" (GZ, 736). When we base ourselves on this great wish, we discover the "priceless jewel" hidden in the robe.

Endo: I have an image of the "priceless jewel" as something like an inexhaustible wellspring of benefit that enables us to get whatever we desire.

Ikeda: When we base ourselves on the great wish for kosen-rufu, all our desires will be realized.

Once at a meeting, after listening with delight to members relate experiences of benefit in faith, President Josei Toda said: "Benefit of the kind mentioned in the experiences given earlier hardly counts as benefit. Supposing the benefit I have received is comparable in size to this auditorium, then their benefit is only the size of a finger."[13] I remember the scene clearly because I attended the meeting and had spoken as a youth division representative.

President Toda had experienced the great and profound benefit of the Mystic Law with his entire being. And he sincerely wanted every Soka Gakkai member without exception to equally gain this great benefit. In these words I could keenly sense his immense mercy.

So he called out, urging us to base our lives on the great wish for kosen-rufu. He told us he wanted to enable us to receive great benefit through working for kosen-rufu. Ultimately, it is we ourselves, not others, who benefit the most from our efforts for kosen-rufu.

Endo: Profound significance then attaches to SGI members' activities.

CHANGING DESTINY INTO MISSION

Ikeda: When we base ourselves on the great wish for kosen-rufu, then everything, every situation, takes on value for our lives. Nothing around us is without meaning; no effort is wasted. The Daishonin cries, "My wish is that all my disciples make a great vow.... Since death is the same in either case, you should be willing to offer your life for the Lotus Sutra. Think of this offering as a drop of dew rejoining the ocean, or a speck of dust returning to the earth" (WND, 1003).

There are also the golden words, "Like dew entering the ocean, or dirt being added to the earth, your good fortune will neither be lost in lifetime after lifetime, nor decay in world after world" (GZ, 968). Life, he says, is as evanescent as dew. In the greater scheme of things, our bodies in and of themselves may seem as insignificant as dust. But by manifesting and acting upon the great vow of faith, our lives become eternal. Our lives, together with the ocean of the Lotus Sutra and the great earth of the Mystic Law, will never for all eternity disappear or decay. We will be forever connected with the great state of life of the Buddha. This is the Daishonin's promise. And this is the dynamic drama we are enacting.

Suda: Speaking of enacting a drama, in "Five Hundred Disciples" there is a passage:

> Inwardly, in secret, the sons act as bodhisattvas,
> but outwardly they show themselves as
> voice-hearers.

They seem to be lessening desires out of hatred
for birth and death,
but in truth they are purifying the Buddha lands.
(LS8, 146)

In other words, outwardly they display the appearance of voice-hearers trying to escape the cycle of birth and death but, in truth, they carry out the practice of bodhisattvas who work to purify the Buddha lands.

Saito: Next, Shakyamuni says:

Before the multitude they seem possessed of the
three poisons
or manifest the signs of heretical views.
My disciples in this manner
use expedient means to save living beings.
(LS8, 146–47)

In other words, the voice-hearers' apparent defilement by the three poisons—greed, anger and stupidity—and attachment to erroneous views are just expedient means they employ to lead all people to enlightenment.

Ikeda: From our standpoint, we have been born in this world to fulfill the "great wish" we have cherished since the remote past. When we have this conviction, we realize that all our sufferings and illusions in this life are expedient means for us to help others become happy.

Were we to appear before others blessed with every good fortune and completely free of suffering, then no one could understand the greatness of the Mystic Law. Furthermore, it is unlikely that we could understand people's hearts. All our karmic sufferings we ourselves dared to choose so that we might overcome them and show proof of victory. We need to be confident of this.

Since these are sufferings that we ourselves created in order to triumph over, our victory is certain. We cannot possibly be defeated.

When we awaken to the great vow of kosen-rufu, that is, when we realize "from the beginning I have been a Buddha," then even harsh destiny changes into mission. We are born with sufferings just like everyone else. By always practicing together with the people, we construct lives of ultimate happiness. This is the drama of mission that we enact.

THE SGI BASES ITSELF ON THE GREAT VOW

Saito: Speaking of turning everything into a source of benefit and value, there is truly a great diversity of people in the SGI. This is because the SGI bases itself not on a narrow, biased small wish but on the great vow for the happiness of all humankind.

Suda: There are leaders who are highly intelligent or enjoy very favorable circumstances or have prestigious academic degrees. Again, there are leaders who, while not having degrees or titles, have had to struggle in life and understand people's hearts more than anybody else. I think that each has a mission and role to play.

Ikeda: That's exactly right. But we mustn't forget that it definitely wasn't intellectuals who worked desperately to rebuild the Soka Gakkai when Japan stood in ruins at the end of the war. The Gakkai was built by down-to-earth, ordinary people. Though widely derided as a "gathering of sick and poor," it was they who constructed the great movement of people united for peace, culture and education that today spans the world.

Intellectuals have certain strengths and they also have weaknesses. Japanese intellectuals, in particular, rather than trying to protect the people, exhibit a strong inclination to try to protect themselves and their own interests. In a life dedicated to the great wish for kosen-rufu, there is no need for such small-mindedness.

It's a matter of discarding the narrow concerns of the lesser self, allowing them to fall away like "a speck of dust returning to the earth" (WND, 1003).

Young people in particular should struggle hard to overcome difficulties with the determination that the greater their struggles, the better they can understand people's hearts and the greater will be their mission.

At any rate, the Lotus Sutra calls out to the voice-hearers and *pratyekabuddhas*: "Return to the wellspring of life!" "Recollect your great vow!" In terms of concrete action, this means living and working among the people. Above all, the Lotus Sutra urges them: "Learn from the people!"

Dostoevsky advises intellectuals, "Let us stand there and let us learn the people's humility, their business-like reasoning, the concreteness of their minds."[14] And he warns them, "Society cannot be animated because you do not rely upon the people; spiritually, the people are not with you, and they are alien to you."[15]

Endo: This was his conviction as someone who lived together with the people during his long exile.

Ikeda: Of particular note, Dostoevsky, who had once discarded his religious beliefs in favor of European liberalism, recouped his spirituality thanks to his experience of living among the people.[16] For Dostoevsky, the people were the great earth that taught him faith in his roots as a human being. It is interesting that, on the day Dostoevsky died, he had his wife read their children the parable of the prodigal son from the Bible.[17]

Endo: The parable of the prodigal son essentially tells the story of a young man who leaves home and squanders his fortune in dissolute living in a distant land and who, upon realizing the error of his ways, repents and returns to his father, where all is forgiven.

Suda: Because of the similarities with the Lotus Sutra's parable of the wealthy man and his poor son (in "Belief and Understanding"), some scholars suggest a connection between the two parables.

Ikeda: Through religious faith, Dostoevsky hoped to bring an end to his spiritual wandering. At the same time, he wanted to bring other wanderers along back with him. He wanted to help them return to the "great earth" of the people, where faith pulses so vibrantly. "Wanderers" correspond to the poor son in the parable of the wealthy man and his poor son, as well as also to the poor man in the parable of the gem in the robe.

In a sense, it could be said that humankind is today in the position of the prodigal son or the poor man. We in the SGI are calling out to humankind, which wanders lost through life: "Here is the great earth of life to which you may return!" "In your heart, you hold the key to bring your wandering to an end!" Such are the lives we are leading. And such actions constitute the true path whereby we may free ourselves from a life of "poverty."

Amid the storm of persecution, Nichiren Daishonin declared: "I, Nichiren, am the richest man in all of present-day Japan. I have dedicated my life to the Lotus Sutra, and my name will be handed down in ages to come" (WND, 268). Let us follow the original Buddha in maintaining this confidence and pride.

NOTES

1. Harrison E. Salisbury, *The 900 Days: The Siege of Leningrad* (New York: Harper and Row, Publishers, 1969), p. 468.

2. Ibid., p. 518.

3. Ibid., p. 460.

4. Ibid., p. 461.

5. Ibid., p. 462.

6. Ibid., p. 463.

7. Hereinafter "Five Hundred Disciples" and "Learners and Adepts," respectively.

8. Translated from Japanese: *Nanden Daizokyo*, ed. Junjiro Takakusu (Tokyo: Taisho Shinshu Daizokyo Kando-kai, 1971), vol. 15, pp. 99–102. Cf. *The Book of Kindred Sayings* (Sanyutta-Nikaya), Part IV, *The Salayatana Book*, trans. Mrs. Rhys Davids (Oxford: The Pali Text Society, 1993), pp. 35–36.

9. Fyodor Dostoevsky, *The Diary of a Writer*, trans. Boris Brasol (New York: Charles Scribner's Sons, 1949), p. 979.

10. Translated from Japanese: Daisaku Ikeda, *Watashino Sobieto Kiko* (My Soviet Travels) (Tokyo: Ushio Shuppansha, 1975), p. 133.

10. Cf. LS8, 150–51.

11. *Words and Phrases of the Lotus Sutra,* vol. 8.

12. At a general meeting of Kamata Chapter at the auditorium of Hoshi University in Tokyo, June 1953.

13. *The Diary of a Writer*, p. 1034.

14. Ibid., p. 1028.

15. Cf. Ibid., p. 984.

17. Aimée Dostoevsky, *Dosutoefushukiden* (Life of Dostoevsky, Japanese edition) (Tokyo: Akagi Shobo, 1946), p. 244.

PART SEVEN

"The Teacher of the Law" Chapter

7 Teachers of the Law
Live Among the People

Suda: An exhibition, which includes two hundred photographs by Rajiv Gandhi, the late former prime minister of India and an avid photographer since childhood, was on display at the Tokyo Fuji Art Museum in Hachioji, Tokyo, in 1996.

Endo: The photos convey a warmth that is beyond words to describe. In particular, the photos of elderly people and children that he took during his travels left me with a sense of his deep love for the Indian people.

Ikeda: Rajiv Gandhi valued the modest handmade items people gave him—shellwork or a basket woven from bamboo—as though they were treasures. I understand he would occasionally take these items out and hold them in his hands with a look of fond reminiscence. Rajiv Gandhi was a leader of conviction. At the same time, he always prized sincerity.

Saito: Speaking before the Japanese Diet in 1985, former Indian Prime Minister Rajiv Gandhi said, "The Buddha's message of compassion is the very condition of human survival in our age."[1] He then met with you, President Ikeda, immediately following this address.

Ikeda: That's right. Although he must have been exhausted, he was smiling and had a look of peace and tranquillity about him. The moment we shook hands, I sensed that behind his gentle countenance was a person of rocklike strength who threw himself 100 percent into achieving his goals.

Saito: That was only a year after the assassination of his mother, Prime Minister Indira Gandhi.

Ikeda: Asked once what was the most important thing she had inherited from her father, Jawaharlal Nehru, Indira Gandhi replied it was her great love for the Indian people. Had Rajiv Gandhi been asked what was the most important thing he received from his mother, his answer would doubtless have been the same.

Not even the terrorist bombing that took his life [in May 1991] could have destroyed the love for the people that burned in Rajiv Gandhi's heart. I believe people have a mission to fulfill that transcends life and death. The lives of those who embrace a mission to which they can wholeheartedly dedicate themselves and even be willing to die for are the most sublime.

Endo: I vividly recall the time you laid a wreath at Rajiv Gandhi's tomb [in February 1992]. In the register of the memorial, you wrote, "There are times when the lives of great leaders seem tragic, but they are actually great, magnificent dramas that serve to eternally awaken the people."

Suda: After Rajiv Gandhi's death, you and Mrs. Ikeda met with his widow, Sonia Gandhi, to console and encourage her. "I really hope that you can change your sad destiny into a cause for realizing an important mission in India," you told her. "Although it may be difficult not to look back, I hope you will keep advancing ever forward. That is the teaching of Shakyamuni Buddha, who was born in this great land of India."

Ikeda: We can change even painful destiny into mission. The Lotus Sutra teaches this strong and resilient way of life. This is what "The

Teacher of the Law" chapter explains when it speaks of the great bodhisattvas who, while capable of being born into pure lands if they so desired, choose instead to be born into impure worlds so that they can expound the Lotus Sutra to help the suffering. We who now spread the Mystic Law in this world are the bodhisattvas to whom the sutra refers. We are enacting a grand drama that we ourselves chose.

This time, let us discuss "The Teacher of the Law" chapter.

THE LOTUS SUTRA WAS EXPOUNDED FOR THE LATTER DAY

> "You should understand that these persons voluntarily relinquish the reward due them for their pure deeds and, in the time after I have passed into extinction, because they pity living beings, they are born in this evil world so they may broadly expound this sutra. If one of these good men or good women in the time after I have passed into extinction is able to secretly expound the Lotus Sutra to one person, even one phrase of it, then you should know that he or she is the envoy of the Thus Come One. He has been dispatched by the Thus Come One and carries out the Thus Come One's work." (LS10, 161-62)

Ikeda: In a sense, all the preceding chapters up to this point have been nothing more than preparation. The most important part of the Lotus Sutra—which represents Shakyamuni's true intent— begins with "The Teacher of the Law" chapter.

Suda: In the progression of events that take place from this chapter on, we see a radical departure from the flow of the preceding chapters. Specifically, in this chapter, Shakyamuni begins discussing the time after his death.

Ikeda: The period after the Buddha's death primarily means the Latter Day of the Law. Shakyamuni addresses how people should live in a time when there is confusion about which teachings are correct and which erroneous.

In the first installment in this series, we described the present as an age lacking philosophy. Who, specifically, will light the way in an "age of darkness" when people cannot see the correct path forward? "The Teacher of the Law" chapter explains in detail the identity of that "person"—in other words, "the teacher of the Law." In modern terms, "the teacher of the Law" could be termed a spiritual leader.

Saito: In light of the overall thrust of this chapter, "teacher of the Law" has a dual meaning. It indicates both one who "makes the Law his master" and one who "becomes a teacher and spreads the Law." These are the two sides of a bodhisattva. "Making the Law one's master" is the aspect of a bodhisattva as a "seeker of the Way." "The teacher who spreads the Law" exemplifies the aspect of a bodhisattva as someone who strives to lead others to enlightenment.

Ikeda: Teachers of the Law unite both of these qualities in themselves. To forget the "seeking" side is to become arrogant; to forget the "saving" side is to become self-centered. While continuing to deepen their own understanding, teachers of the Law lead others to happiness; and through helping others become happy, they further deepen their understanding. Seeking the Law is itself leading others to enlightenment; and leading others to enlightenment is itself seeking the Law. Herein lies the supreme path in life.

Saito: That this is a path for all people is the key point, isn't it? In this chapter, the distinction between lay people, on the one hand, and monks and nuns, on the other, is revealed as completely irrelevant. In one place, it speaks of "the lay persons or monks or nuns who read and recite the Lotus Sutra" (LS10, 162). As this suggests, the identity of the teacher of the Law transcends distinctions between clerics and laypeople.

Nichiren Shoshu priests assert, among other things, that priests are inherently superior to lay believers. It is patently obvious, however, that such a discriminatory attitude goes completely against the words of the Lotus Sutra.

Endo: The teachers of the Law expound the Lotus Sutra to others while themselves upholding, reading and reciting the sutra. Their practice comes down to continually talking with people and enabling them to hear about the Lotus Sutra.

Ikeda: In a sense, it is a struggle of words, a campaign of dialogue. Our movement to conduct dialogue truly accords with the spirit of "The Teacher of the Law" chapter.

Shakyamuni spent his entire life, until the day he died, talking with people. Nichiren Daishonin, similarly, in addition to his efforts at dialogue, left behind a vast body of writings held to be larger than that of any Japanese person of his day. He wrote and spoke exhaustively and because of his noble efforts later generations can learn the teachings he expounded.

It is a battle of words. Words illuminate not only the time when they are uttered or set down but future ages as well. In the hope of leaving behind something of value for future generations, I give speeches on Buddhism and hold dialogues with world leaders.

Endo: In the preceding eight chapters—from the second, "Expedient Means," through the ninth, "Prophecies Conferred on Learners and Adepts"—Shakyamuni's central concern is to enable his present disciples to attain Buddhahood. As a result of his preaching in these chapters, all of the voice-hearers enter the path of attaining Buddhahood. In other words, in his preaching up to and including the "Learners and Adepts" chapter, Shakyamuni confirms that his immediate disciples will all attain supreme enlightenment. In that sense, the preaching in these chapters is for Shakyamuni's contemporaries.

Ikeda: That is certainly how these eight chapters look on the surface. But viewed in the context of the entire Lotus Sutra, it becomes apparent that these eight chapters are also in fact for the age after the Buddha's passing.

Actually, not just these eight chapters but the entire Lotus Sutra is for the time after the Buddha's death. Nichiren Daishonin says that the Lotus Sutra's theoretical teaching (or first half) appears to have been expounded for the voice-hearer disciples who were Shakyamuni's contemporaries. On a deeper level, however, he explains, it, like the Lotus Sutra's essential teaching (or latter half), was taught for people after the Buddha's passing, for the people of the Latter Day (cf. WND, 369).

Shakyamuni's lifetime in India was short, but the period after his passing is long. Shakyamuni's followers in his day were few, but the people in the world after his passing are innumerable. In his immense compassion, the Buddha naturally wanted to lead all people to enlightenment, so the people after his passing was his primary focus.

The teachers of the Law embody this immense compassion of the Buddha and take action accordingly. They are the "envoys of the Thus Come One" (LS10, 162).

Endo: That's why the portion of the sutra from "The Teacher of the Law" chapter on is so important. According to Nichiren Daishonin, the five chapters from "The Teacher of the Law" through "Peaceful Practices" explain how ordinary people of the Latter Day should practice the teaching of the one Buddha vehicle that the preceding eight chapters reveal.

Nichiren Daishonin writes in the Gosho:

> The eight chapters beginning with "Expedient Means"
> and continuing through "Prophecies" are concerned

primarily with clarifying how persons of the two vehicles [voice-hearers and *pratyekabuddhas*] can attain
Buddhahood, and secondarily with clarifying how
bodhisattvas and ordinary people can attain Buddhahood.

The following five chapters, the "Teacher of the
Law," "Treasure Tower," "Devadatta," "Encouraging
Devotion," and "Peaceful Practices" chapters, explain
how the teachings set forth in the preceding eight chapters are to be carried out by ordinary persons in the latter age. (WND, 91)

Ikeda: "Ordinary persons in a latter age" indicates Nichiren Daishonin and all of his followers.

In his writings, the Daishonin quotes extensively from the five
chapters beginning with "Teacher of the Law." And within the
Lotus Sutra itself, from "The Teacher of the Law" chapter on,
there are a great many references to the time after the Buddha's
passing.

What we should note here is that Nichiren Daishonin, more
than anyone else, perfectly matched in his conduct the sutra's
description of the "votary of the Lotus Sutra" who will appear in
the Latter Day of the Law. From another standpoint, in light of the
fact that Nichiren Daishonin read the Lotus Sutra with his life, it
could be said that the Lotus Sutra was expounded to prepare the
way for the Daishonin.

The Daishonin asserts that Nam-myoho-renge-kyo, the "one
fundamental Law" through which all Buddhas attain enlightenment, is itself the essence of the Lotus Sutra and the great teaching that can enable all people of the Latter Day to attain
enlightenment.

Saito: In that light, we can see why in "The Teacher of the Law,"
Shakyamuni says that offerings should be made to the teachers of
the Law such as would be made to the Buddha (cf. LS10, 161, 163).

The Sanskrit text of the sutra is still more explicit, explaining that these teachers of the Law "should be viewed as Buddhas" and are "equal to the Thus Come One."

Suda: The Lotus Sutra also explains that the teachers of the Law are "envoys of the Thus Come One" who have been dispatched by the Buddha and who carry out the Buddha's work (cf. LS10, 161–62). "Envoys of the Thus Come One" is an important term that the Daishonin uses time and again.

Also, the offense of uttering even a single word of slander against these teachers of the Law is even greater than that of continually slandering the Buddha to his face for the duration of an entire *kalpa.* On the other hand, the sutra explains that the benefit of praising the teachers of the Law surpasses that of praising the Buddha with countless verses for one *kalpa.*

Ikeda: In part, this is because the Law, not the Buddha, is the fundamental cause for attaining Buddhahood and should be cherished accordingly. The Lotus Sutra is the teaching that explains the fundamental Law through which all Buddhas—including Shakyamuni—attain enlightenment. And the teachers of the Law in the Latter Day expound the teaching that is the true cause for attaining Buddhahood.

Endo: The relationship between the Law and the Buddha is the relationship between "that which gives birth" and "that to which birth is given."

Ikeda: Nichiren Daishonin characterizes this Law as the "ultimate principle of compassion." In the Gosho, "Chanting the daimoku of the Lotus Sutra," the Daishonin writes: "All Buddhas and bodhisattvas are our compassionate parents. You should understand that the ultimate principle of compassion that these Buddhas and bodhisattvas use to instruct living beings is contained nowhere but in the Lotus Sutra.... This is the reason why the Lotus Sutra is superior to all other sutras" (GZ, 9).

The Lotus Sutra surpasses all other sutras because it contains the Law of Nam-myoho-renge-kyo — the "ultimate principle of compassion." It is the great teaching of compassion that can lead all people to enlightenment. As the "Teacher of the Law" chapter says, "the Lotus is the foremost!" (LS10, 164).

Endo: That's what the well-known passage about the Lotus Sutra surpassing all teachings in the past, present and future indicates.

"The sutras I have preached number immeasurable thousands, ten thousands, millions. Among the sutras I have preached, now preach, and will preach, this Lotus Sutra is the most difficult to believe and the most difficult to understand" (LS10, 164).

Saito: In that sense, the "envoys of the Thus Come One" are "envoys of compassion." The teachers of the Law put into practice the Buddha's immense spirit of compassion while embracing, reading, reciting, expounding and copying the Lotus Sutra (i.e., carrying out the five practices that the sutra itself prescribes). In the Latter Day, however, embracing the Law is itself enlightenment; in other words, all these practices are included in the one practice of embracing faith in the Gohonzon.

Ikeda: Embracing faith in the Gohonzon means living with the spirit of the Buddha and dedicating one's life to the Buddha's vow to lead all people to enlightenment. That is the fundamental meaning of "embracing the Lotus Sutra" and of the five kinds of practices. It's not a matter of literally holding, reading and reciting the scrolls of the Lotus Sutra and expounding upon their meaning. Rather, the point is to inherit the Buddha's spirit and to thoroughly manifest the Buddha's compassion in one's life.

Ultimately, Shakyamuni's purpose in bestowing prophecies of enlightenment upon the voice-hearers in the preceding chapters is to cause them to arouse the "same spirit as the Buddha." Those who put that spirit into practice after the Buddha's death are teachers of the Law.

SHAKUBUKU MEANS SPEAKING THE TRUTH

Saito: On the matter of propagation, I've recently received a number of questions from new Soka Gakkai members on the difference between *shoju* and *shakubuku* methods. Many people, it seems, have the impression that *shakubuku* means using strong words whereas *shoju* means assuming a gentle manner.

Ikeda: It is a great mistake to suppose that *shakubuku* means trying to force someone to take faith. Doing *shakubuku* essentially means speaking the truth. Since the Lotus Sutra explains the truth, it is called the "sutra of *shakubuku*."

Now, in the Latter Day of the Law, all our efforts to tell people about and spread Nam-myoho-renge-kyo—the essence of the Lotus Sutra—constitute *shakubuku*. In house-cleaning, for example, it doesn't matter whether one cleans vigorously or at a leisurely pace as long as the main objective of a clean house is realized.

Suda: People probably suppose that *shakubuku* has to be harsh because of the somewhat alarming image one gets from the Chinese characters with which the term is written [a combination of two ideograms meaning "break" and "restrain"].

Ikeda: Shakubuku does not mean going out to pick a fight. *Shakubuku*, sharing the teachings of the Daishonin's Buddhism with others, has to be of thoroughgoing compassion. Josei Toda, the second Soka Gakkai president, once said:

> We should do abundant *shakubuku* out of sincere conviction in the Daishonin's teaching. And in so doing, we

should not harbor feelings of antipathy toward others. We should not get into angry disputes. All we need to do is teach people earnestly and gently. The important thing is that we have this spirit to teach. If someone opposes or attacks us, then that person will suffer the consequences of his or her actions. It is important to share Buddhism with a spirit of compassion. It's almost like being in love.[2]

President Toda certainly had a way of putting things! When people are in love, they go all out. They go through many sheets of stationery writing and rewriting letters. They stay up all night thinking about the words they will use to invite the other person out on their next day off. If everything goes well, they might decide to get married. Unlike marriage sometimes, however, *shakubuku* will never cause one to have regrets!

Endo: I think we can say that Shakyamuni's method of preaching was to teach people gently. Shakyamuni first expounded the doctrine of the "true entity of all phenomena" in an attempt to help people grasp the truth that everyone can become a Buddha. When Shakyamuni revealed this teaching, Shariputra alone understood, while others did not.

And so Shakyamuni related various similes and parables. As a result, the four leaders of the voice-hearers came to understand. Because many still had not yet grasped his meaning, however, Shakyamuni next explained his profound relationship with them from the distant past. Through this revelation, all of the voice-hearers could finally accept and understand his teaching.

Thus, Shakyamuni racked his mind to find a way to clarify his teaching so that all people could comprehend it. He did not abandon people because they were slow to understand. He had the deep wish, and the tenacity of purpose, to enable all people to become Buddhas, no matter how much effort it required on his part.

Suda: That is the very spirit that motivates our practice of *shakubuku* today.

Ikeda: Yes. The key point is to pray that your sincerity will be understood by the other person. Wisdom arises from prayer. Prayer gives birth to confidence and joy.

While *shakubuku* is difficult, when we bear in mind that, through our actions, both the other person and we ourselves will definitely realize tremendous happiness and benefit, nothing could be more joyful. Mr. Toda often said: "We should not agonize over doing *shakubuku*. We have to do *shakubuku* with a sense of joy."[3]

In practice, while some will immediately believe and understand the Daishonin's Buddhism, there will of course be those for whom this will not be the case. But there is no need to be impatient. Whatever the immediate outcome of our efforts, there is absolutely no doubt about the benefit we receive from having offered earnest prayer and made the effort to conduct dialogue about our Buddhist faith. And precisely because *shakubuku* is not easy, it affords us opportunities to tap our innate wisdom and grow. If we plant a seed, in time it will definitely flower.

The key point, it seems to me, is to talk to people with a sense of joy and exhilaration to be serving as the Buddha's envoy.

Endo: I think it's also important to warmly praise those doing *shakubuku*.

Ikeda: That's right. Those carrying out this practice are "envoys of the Thus Come One"; they should be respected as Buddhas. This is the spirit of "The Teacher of the Law" chapter. Those who have the spirit to praise others accumulate good fortune and strength and as a result can lead many to happiness.

SGI members who dedicate their lives to kosen-rufu should be treasured as Buddhas. When we understand this spirit, we understand not only "The Teacher of the Law" chapter but the entire Lotus Sutra.

The Three Rules of Preaching: Robe, Seat and Room

1) The "Room of Compassion"

Endo: In "The Teacher of the Law" chapter, Shakyamuni explains the manner of propagation after his death in terms of the "three rules of preaching of robe, seat and room":

> "Medicine King, if there are good men and good women who, after the Thus Come One has entered extinction, wish to expound this Lotus Sutra for the four kinds of believers, how should they expound it? These good men and good women should enter the Thus Come One's room, put on the Thus Come One's robe, sit in the Thus Come One's seat, and then for the sake of the four kinds of believers broadly expound this sutra.
>
> "The 'Thus Come One's room' is the state of mind that shows great pity and compassion toward all living beings. The 'Thus Come One's robe' is the mind that is gentle and forbearing. The 'Thus Come One's seat' is the emptiness of all phenomena. (LS10, 166)

Ikeda: This is highly poetic. Shakyamuni uses the images of "robe," "seat" and "room" to clarify the Buddha's spirit in expounding the Lotus Sutra. And he urges people to broadly expound the teaching, saying in effect, "If you base yourselves on this spirit, then, even if you encounter difficulties, you can lead people to enlightenment unerringly just as the Buddha does."

Why, then, is the Buddha's great compassion compared to a room?

Saito: Compassion in the Buddhist sense is pity and profound affection. Feeling compassion toward others means sensing a common humanity or kinship, a bond as fellow living beings. This could also be called "love," but it is not egoistic love of the kind that can readily devolve into hate. It is love of humanity rooted in profound insight into the nature of life and existence. It could also be thought of as a true sense of solidarity arising from a shared aspiration for mutual happiness and growth.

Suda: Compassion is also the spirit to share others' sufferings, to empathize with them in their sorrows. If we see someone suffering, compassion impels us to extend the person a helping hand, to share his or her pain. It is a profound emotion of that kind.

Ikeda: In terms of our stance vis-á-vis others, an attitude of compassion does not mean looking down on someone from a position of superiority. It is not a vertical but a horizontal relationship. It is a feeling of sympathy toward others as fellow human beings. And it is based on respect.

That's why it's called the "room of compassion." We invite a friend into a compassionate life-space and warmly embrace them; we sit down in the same room and discuss life as equals. We discuss things and learn from one another as fellow human beings, and together we strive to improve our lives. Creating such a warm and welcoming space for dialogue and exchange is in itself *shakubuku.*

Endo: If we approach someone with the arrogant attitude that we are going to "save" the person, it will only provoke a negative response.

Ikeda: In "On Establishing the Correct Teaching for the Peace of the Land," Nichiren Daishonin calls the "host" who engages the "guest" in dialogue a "friend in the orchid room" (WND, 23). When someone spends time in a room filled with orchids, the fragrance of the flowers naturally permeates clothing. Similarly, dialogue should be conducted in such a way that the other person is imbued with the "fragrance of compassion."

Propagation does not mean trying to force something on someone, nor is it for the sake of the organization. Propagation is an act of venerating the Buddha nature in the lives of others. Therefore, our efforts in *shakubuku* should be motivated by a spirit of the greatest respect for the other person.

President Toda said, "The basis for doing *shakubuku* is a feeling of sympathy for others' sufferings." Compassion, in other words, is fundamental. You don't propagate Buddhism with a confrontational spirit of trying to refute someone's ideas and win the person over to your own side.

Suda: Since it's a matter of conducting dialogue, we have to listen to what the other person has to say. Yet there are those who talk on and on, monopolizing the conversation, and then suppose that they have had a dialogue.

Ikeda: It can't be called a dialogue where one person constantly interrupts while the other is trying to express an opinion and then lays down sweeping conclusions.

Even if you think that what someone is saying is a bit odd, rather than constantly raising objections, you should have the broad-mindedness to try to understand his or her point of view. Then the person will feel secure and can listen to what you have to say.

In that sense, the Buddha is truly a master at dialogue. Shakyamuni and the Daishonin had such heartwarming personalities that just meeting them must have given people a sense of immense delight. And that's probably why so many took such pleasure in listening to their words.

Suda: The "room of compassion" conveys an image of such warmth and breadth of character.

Ikeda: In this connection, there is a certain incident involving Shakyamuni.[4] A man named Upali, who believed in Jainism,[5] once tried to defeat Shakyamuni in debate. But he was so moved by Shakyamuni's character and wisdom that he wound up asking to become the Buddha's disciple.

Shakyamuni, rather than exulting at his having won Upali's admiration, admonished the latter, saying: "You should not so lightly cast aside the beliefs that you have held up to now. Please think the matter over carefully."

Upali, impressed all the more by this response, answered, "In society, it is rumored that the monk Gautama [Shakyamuni] says that people should make offerings to him and not make offerings to others; and asserts that whereas making offerings to him and his disciples confers benefit, there is no benefit to be gained from making offerings to others. But in reality, the attitude of the World-Honored One is completely the opposite. I will devote myself to the Buddha's teachings with increased ardor."

Hearing about Upali's conversion, a Jainist leader accompanied by a number of his followers went to Upali's house. Upali received them cordially. But the leader rebuked him saying, "You're like a fool who goes for wool and comes home shorn." With great politeness, Upali patiently explained, "If it should be someone like Shakyamuni by whom I should be led astray, I could desire nothing more. If the royal families and Brahmans, peasants and slaves throughout the world could be so led astray by Shakyamuni, there would be eternal peace and happiness throughout the world."

2) The "Robe of Gentleness and Forbearance"

Suda: Continuing, it is easy to see why the Buddha's "robe" is a metaphor for a "mind that is gentle and forbearing." Just as a robe protects one's body from cold and heat, when we don the robe of gentleness and forbearance, we are not shaken by hardships or difficulties.

Ikeda: That's right. In our propagation efforts, remaining undaunted in the face of obstacles is very important. With these words, Shakyamuni is urging his followers to maintain a radiant and composed state of mind, no matter what pressures might be brought to bear against them.

In seeking to propagate Buddhism after the Buddha's passing, difficulties are inevitable. Therefore, it is necessary that we have a spirit of forbearance and patience. We need a spirit to endure. Enduring is neither retreating nor conceding defeat. We have to persevere and win. No matter what happens, we must not become disheartened. Kosen-rufu is a struggle of the spirit. Those who allow themselves to be inwardly defeated cannot be said to possess forbearance.

Saito: In "The Selection of the Time," Nichiren Daishonin says, "Even if it seems that, because I was born in the ruler's domain, I follow him in my actions, I will never follow him in the beliefs of my heart" (WND, 579). By saying that he must "follow the ruler" in his actions, the Daishonin means that he has to endure persecution. By "I will never follow him in the beliefs of my heart," he indicates that in his heart he is not defeated.

Ikeda: That is the spirit of forbearance. When the Daishonin was condemned to be exiled to desolate Sado Island, physically he abided by the government's decree. But in his heart he possessed the vast state of life to be able to say, "I feel immeasurable delight even though I am now an exile" (WND, 386).

A spirit of patience generates the greatest strength. If one has true courage one can endure any hardship. In "Encouraging Devotion," the thirteenth chapter, the metaphor "armor of perseverance" (LS13, 194) is used to describe that strength. "One Who Can Forbear" is another name for Buddha. Both Shakyamuni and Nichiren Daishonin had tremendous powers of patience and forbearance.

Endo: "The Teacher of the Law" chapter emphasizes that the teachers of the Law will encounter persecution. The passage that the Daishonin read with his life, "since hatred and jealousy toward this sutra abound even when the Thus Come One is in the world, how much more will this be so after his passing?" (LS10, 164), is also found in this chapter.

Suda: This explains that the teachers of the Law meet with persecution because the Lotus Sutra is difficult to believe and difficult to understand. Because it is difficult to believe and understand, it aroused hatred and jealousy even in Shakyamuni's day. This passage indicates that persecution will be even worse in the future.

Ikeda: It says, "how much more will this be so after his passing?" Why should there be more persecution after the Buddha's passing than while he is alive?

"After his passing" refers to a time when the Buddha's spirit has been forgotten and there is great turmoil and confusion in areas of religion and philosophy. In such an age, while people might appear to revere the Buddha, they forget the Buddha's essential spirit; and while there are Buddhist schools, the spirit of the Buddha does not abide in them. In such a time, while there may be religions, they exist for the sake of religion and not for human beings. The Lotus Sutra was taught especially for the people of such an age.

The teachers of the Law propagate the Lotus Sutra, which conveys the Buddha's spirit, in an age that has completely forgotten the spirit of the Buddha. Consequently, there is much hatred and jealousy toward them. In an age that has lost sight of humanity, it is no easy undertaking to campaign for a restoration of humanity.

Suda: In that sense, those who experience no difficulties are not truly propagating the Law. The Nichiren Shoshu priesthood, for example, has never — either now or during the war — been persecuted.

By contrast, from the time of its first president, Tsunesaburo Makiguchi, to the present, the Soka Gakkai has been repeatedly attacked and persecuted. Truly, we are reading the Lotus Sutra with our lives. This is proof that our organization is indeed putting the spirit of the Buddha into practice.

Saito: Persecutions are always occasioned by scheming. In Shakyamuni's day, there was an unending succession of scandals stemming from fabrications and misrepresentations by those of malicious intent. To obliterate the Buddhist order, some heinous individuals went so far as to commit murder and then try to pin the blame on Shakyamuni's followers.

Suda: In Nichiren Daishonin's case, Nembutsu followers and others committed murders and arson in Kamakura, the capital, and then spread rumors that these crimes were the work of the Daishonin's followers. This resulted in the Daishonin being exiled to Sado Island. The Daishonin's followers were suppressed because those hostile to their activities had made them appear a dangerous order. In any age, there is a similar pattern of persecution against those who uphold the correct Buddhist teaching.

Endo: Therefore, we cannot discard the "robe of forbearance."

Ikeda: Allow me to share another anecdote.[6] Once there was a Brahman who was upset that his wife had become Shakyamuni's follower. Since his wife praised the Buddha so highly, he went to try to defeat him in debate. But instead of refuting Shakyamuni, the Brahman was so impressed by his preaching that he converted to Buddhism himself. His fellow Brahmans thought this scandalous. They stormed into the Jetavana Monastery and there heaped curses and abuse on Shakyamuni. What do you suppose Shakyamuni did in response?

Shakyamuni asked one of the Brahmans, "If a relative or friend came to your house, would you welcome him as a guest?"

"That's right," the Brahman replied. "I sometimes entertain guests."

"If the person does not accept the food that is provided for him, then to whom does it belong?" Shakyamuni continued.

"It naturally belongs to me, the head of the household."

"In the same way," Shakyamuni said, "if I do not accept the abuses that you hurl at me, then will not these return to you and become your own?

Suda: He certainly knew how to touch a sensitive nerve with gentleness and forbearance!

Endo: When we put on the "robe of gentleness and forbearance," our hearts become impervious to negative words.

Saito: And to the extent that such words do not enter our hearts, they return to the people who uttered them in the first place, causing them to suffer.

3) The "Seat of the Emptiness of All Phenomena"

Endo: Third, what is meant by "The 'Thus Come One's seat' is the emptiness of all phenomena?"

Ikeda: This refers to the Buddha's unrestricted wisdom. Everything is constantly undergoing change. All existence is impermanent, nonsubstantial. The "Thus Come One's seat" indicates the Buddha's capacity to correctly perceive the true entity of all phenomena in the world and his state of life that nothing can sway or upset.

Suda: This is easy to understand theoretically, but actually achieving such a state is no easy matter.

Ikeda: The Daishonin says: "The 'seat' means carrying out religious practice 'without begrudging one's life.' By carrying out such practice, one awakens to the 'emptiness of all phenomena'" (GZ, 737). Sitting in the seat of the emptiness of all phenomena, in other words, means taking selfless action.

People tend to become attached to or caught up in various things. For example, they may be captivated by fame and social standing. Once they acquire these, they are loath to surrender them. And in some respects, that people behave in this way may be only natural. To sit in the seat of the emptiness of all phenomena, however, means daring to overcome these egoistic attachments and selflessly exert oneself in faith, to devote one's life to kosen-rufu. The ultimate meaning of "emptiness" or "nonsubstantiality" is found in such faith.

This, of course, doesn't mean treating our lives carelessly or thoughtlessly. Rather, it means using our precious lives ungrudgingly for the sake of Buddhism.

Saito: From such a dedicated, selfless spirit arises the wisdom to help people become happy.

Ikeda: Exactly. A person of selfless dedication is one who can help others. I once asked President Toda, "When we do *shakubuku*, are we in a sense doing *shakubuku* to ourselves?"

He replied: "The point is that Nam-myoho-renge-kyo is the very wellspring of our lives. Unless we have that realization, we cannot do true *shakubuku*. There isn't any special technique or method for doing *shakubuku*. In the Latter Day, *shakubuku* is a matter of determining: 'Nam-myoho-renge-kyo is the sum and essence of my being!'"[7]

He also once said, "The ultimate *shakubuku* is to determine that one's life itself is Nam-myoho-renge-kyo." President Toda spoke these words with a resolute tone; it was the voice of someone who deeply wanted to help young people understand the truth.

"Determining that one's life is Nam-myoho-renge-kyo" beautifully expresses the principle of the emptiness of all phenomena and the spirit of not begrudging one's life. I hope that all of you, with these words as your guide, will earnestly pursue the essence of faith. For it is this pursuit that constitutes true Buddhist study.

THE PRACTICE OF COMPASSION, FORBEARANCE AND WISDOM

Suda: We have discussed the three rules of preaching of robe, seat and room. The fact that the teacher of the Law dwells in the room of the Thus Come One, wears the robe of the Thus Come One and sits in the seat of the Thus Come One suggests that the teacher of the Law is equal to the Thus Come One.

Also it seems that, just as an ambassador of a country enacts that country's will, we could consider the actions of the "envoy of the Thus Come One" as equivalent to those of the Buddha.

Ikeda: That's a good analogy.

Saito: Don't these three rules also express virtues of the Buddha that teachers of the Law acquire by dedicating themselves to the great wish for the Lotus Sutra's propagation?

Ikeda: We can indeed understand the three rules in those terms. Nichiren Daishonin says: "The robe, seat and room represent the Buddha's three bodies of the Dharma body, the reward body and the manifested body; the three truths of nonsubstantiality, temporary existence and the Middle Way; and the three categories of action of deed, word and thought" (GZ, 737).

The Dharma body, bliss body and manifested body are the Buddha's virtues. Simply put, they correspond to truth, wisdom and compassion. Teachers of the Law are endowed with these virtues.

The Daishonin also says, "Now Nichiren and his followers who chant Nam-myoho-renge-kyo are fulfilling the three rules [of preaching represented by robe, seat and room] each moment of their lives" (GZ, 737). In other words, through the practice of chanting and propagating the daimoku of Nam-myoho-renge-kyo, we attain the Buddha's virtues. We acquire these virtues through our determination in faith.

Even if we have no special ability, the important point is that our hearts brim with the joy of chanting the Mystic Law and the joy of sharing the Mystic Law with others. Such joyful faith incorporates the rules of robe, seat and room, as well as the virtues of compassion, gentleness and wisdom.

Saito: "The Teacher of the Law" chapter stresses the importance of "for a moment thinking of the Lotus Sutra with joy" (cf. LS10, 160). It goes so far as to say that all people can attain Buddhahood if they simply hear about the Mystic Law and feel delight.

It also states, "these persons [teachers of the Law] delight in expounding the Law. And if one listens to them for even a moment, he or she will immediately attain the ultimate anuttara-samyak-sambodhi" (LS10, 162). *Anuttara-samyak-sambodhi* is a Sanskrit term meaning the Buddha's enlightenment.

Ikeda: A teacher of the Law is originally a person who has heard the Lotus Sutra and felt delight. Others hear that teacher of the Law expound the Lotus Sutra and they, too, feel delight. The eternal path of attaining Buddhahood is thus a kind of chain reaction of joy.

Nichiren Daishonin says:

> When I, Nichiren, first took faith in the Lotus Sutra, I was like a single drop of water or a single particle of dust in all the country of Japan. But later, when two people, three people, ten people, and eventually a hundred, a thousand, ten thousand, and a million people come to recite the Lotus Sutra and transmit it to others, then they will form a Mount Sumeru of perfect enlightenment,[8] an ocean of great nirvana! Seek no other path by which to attain Buddhahood! (WND, 580)

The SGI acts in exact accord with these words.

Saito: At the start of this discussion, you described the teacher of the Law as a spiritual leader who illuminates society in an age lacking philosophy. I think it's wonderful that in the SGI we believe that the people themselves are teachers of the Law.

Endo: In many established religions, the members of the clergy carry out propagation. Religious propagation often takes place at large gatherings; I hear that in the United States, there is a great deal of proselytizing on television.

By contrast, the way of the SGI is propagation by the people and for the people. Small gatherings such as discussion meetings are the main avenue for spreading the Daishonin's Buddhism, and the method is that of one-on-one dialogue. I think that this will become the pattern of propagation for religions in the twenty-first century.

Suda: Dr. Bryan Wilson, former president of the International Society of Religion, remarked in his dialogue with you, President Ikeda:

> Personal contact certainly appears to be the most effective technique of mission [i.e., propagation of faith],...
> In a world in which everyone learns to grow cynical, for example, about advertising, the fact of personal genuineness may in itself be so refreshing that the message is more adequately communicated even by a relatively ignorant missionary than by a technically adroit media advertisement with absolutely authoritative information.[9]

Ikeda: That's right. It comes down to authenticity. Eloquence is not what matters. The important thing in propagation is genuine sincerity. President Toda often said, "When you do *shakubuku* you create lasting trust."

Those Who Spread
the Mystic Law Are Noble

Endo: When we consider the teachers of the Law in this light, we see that they deliberately, out of their compassion, seek to be born in an evil age.

Ikeda: "The Teacher of the Law" chapter says that these envoys of the Buddha "freely choose where they will be born" (LS10, 163). Nichiren Daishonin explains that someone who attains Buddhahood immediately returns to the realm of the nine worlds and again freely engages in efforts to lead people to enlightenment.

In the Gosho "The Ultimate Teaching Affirmed by All Buddhas of Past, Present and Future," the Daishonin says:

> Reaching the supreme Land of Tranquil Light unimpeded, in the space of a moment one will return to the midst of the dream of birth and death in the nine worlds. One's body pervades the Dharma worlds in the ten directions and one's mind enters the lives of all sentient beings. Impelled from within and drawn from without, in the harmony of [internal] cause and [external] relation, one freely exercises the transcendental power of compassion and widely brings benefit to living beings without any impediment." (GZ, 574)

We willed ourselves to be born in this world of suffering. The Daishonin says, "Now Nichiren and his followers who chant Nam-myoho-renge-kyo are great teachers among teachers" (GZ, 736). SGI members who make the Daishonin's spirit their own and dedicate themselves to achieving kosen-rufu are "great teachers of the Law among teachers." When our present lives come to an end, we are reborn in this world "in the space of a moment."

We might picture it something like this: We struggle hard in this life and then go to Eagle Peak. There, somewhat winded after the journey, we report to the Daishonin: "I've come having fulfilled my mission!"

The Daishonin commends us: "Good work! You really did a fine job!" He then asks, "Well, where do you want to go next?" There's no time to even think about taking it easy for a while. Of course, those who really want to relax can do so! We're completely free.

As the Daishonin indicates when he speaks of freely exercising the "transcendental power of compassion," out of compassion, in an instant we return in vigorous spirits to a new sphere of mission. Death and rebirth are like going to sleep one day and waking up the next morning.

Suda: Out of pity and sympathy for those suffering, the teachers of the Law yearn to be born in an impure world. The Great Teacher Miao-lo of China calls this "deliberately creating the appropriate karma." The teachers of the Law are people who, because of the benefit they have accumulated from their Buddhist practice, could by rights be born in a "good land." But they deliberately create the negative karma to be born in a world rife with evil so that they can spread Buddhism.

Ikeda: President Toda often said: "Someone who is too exemplary from the outset cannot go among the people. To spread Buddhism, we intentionally chose to be born as people who are poor or sick." "Life is like appearing in a play," he would say.

He also said, "I lost my wife, and my daughter died. My business failed. Because I have known such suffering, I could become president of the Soka Gakkai." People who have not experienced painful struggles or suffering cannot understand the hearts of others. Only if one has tasted life's bitterness can one lead people to happiness.

To simply view your sufferings as "karma" is backward-looking. We should have the attitude: "These are sufferings I took on for the sake of my mission. I vowed to overcome these problems through faith."

When we understand this principle of "deliberately creating the appropriate karma," our frame of mind is transformed; what we had previously viewed as destiny, we come to see as mission. There is absolutely no way we cannot overcome sufferings that are the result of a vow that we ourselves made.

Saito: Nichiren Daishonin comments on the passage, "such persons...have fulfilled their great vow, and because they take pity on living beings they have been born in this human world.... where they may broadly expound...the Lotus Sutra of the Wonderful Law" (LS10, 161). He says:

> The "great vow" refers to the propagation of the Lotus Sutra. "Living beings" refers to all beings in the country of Japan. The persons who "are born in this human world" are Nichiren and his followers. "Broadly" means to expound the sutra throughout the southern continent of Jambudvipa [i.e., the entire world]. "This sutra" refers to the daimoku. Now it is Nichiren and his followers who chant the daimoku, Nam-myoho-renge-kyo. (GZ, 736)

The SGI members who are spreading the Mystic Law throughout the world truly accumulate immeasurable good fortune. They are genuine followers of the original Buddha who are born in this world to accomplish their mission for kosen-rufu.

Ikeda: Therefore, we should all respect one another as noble beings each with a profound mission to fulfill. At the outset we talked about India. Mahatma Gandhi, the father of modern India, once said: "I do not want to be reborn, but if I have to be reborn I should be reborn an untouchable so that I may share their sorrows, sufferings, and the affronts leveled against them in order that I may endeavor to free myself and them from their miserable condition."[10]

In these sentiments, I sense something akin to the spirit of "deliberately creating the appropriate karma." It's a matter of compassion, of living for and together with others. It is the desire to be born among those who are suffering the most.

The Buddha is to be found among those suffering the most. Buddhism exists to enable those suffering the most to become the happiest. "The Teacher of the Law" chapter explains the sublime temperament of spiritual leaders who devote themselves to, and live out their lives among, the people.

NOTES

1. "Address to the Joint Session of the Japanese Diet," Tokyo, November 29, 1985.

2. *Toda Josei Zenshu* (Collected Writings of Josei Toda) (Tokyo: Seikyo Shimbunsha, 1982), vol. 2, p. 466.

3. *Toda Josei Zenshu*, p. 120.

4. This episode and related dialogue are translated from Japanese: *Nanden Daizokyo*, ed., Junjiro Takakusu (Tokyo: Taisho Shinshu Daizokyo Kanko-kai, 1971), vol. 10, pp. 140–56. cf. *The Collection of the Middle Length Sayings* (Majjhima-Nikaya), vol. II, trans. I.B. Horner (Oxford: The Pali Text Society, 1994), pp. 38–49.

5. Jainism: An Indian religion that stresses nonviolence and not killing any forms of life, and teaches the liberation of the soul by right knowledge, right faith and right conduct.

6. This episode and related dialogue are translated from Japanese: *Nanden Daizokyo*, ed., Junjiro Takakusu (Tokyo: Taisho Shinshu Daizokyo Kanko-kai, 1971), vol. 12, pp. 276–77. cf. *The Book of Kindred Sayings* (Sanyutta-Nikaya), Part I, trans. Mrs. Rhys Davids (Oxford: The Pali Text Society, 1993), pp. 201–2.

7. *Toda Josei Zenshu*, pp. 466–67.

8. Wonderful enlightenment: *Myogaku*, the last of the fifty-two stages of bodhisattva practice, indicating the state of Buddhahood.

9. Daisaku Ikeda and Bryan Wilson, *Human Values in a Changing World* (Secaucus, NJ: Lyle Stuart Inc., 1987), p. 132.

10. Louis Fischer, *The Life of Mahatma Gandhi* (New York: Harper and Brothers, Publishers, 1950), p. 144.

Glossary

anuttara-samyak-sambodhi (Skt) Supreme perfect enlightenment, the enlightenment of a Buddha.

asamkhya See *nayuta*.

bodhisattva (Skt) A being who aspires to attain Buddhahood and carries out altruistic practices to achieve that goal. Compassion predominates in bodhisattvas, who postpone their own entry into nirvana in order to lead others toward enlightenment.

Bodhisattvas of the Earth Those who chant and propagate Nam-myoho-renge-kyo. *Earth* indicates the enlightened nature of all people. The term describes the innumerable bodhisattvas who appear in the "Emerging from the Earth" chapter of the Lotus Sutra and are entrusted by Shakyamuni with the task of propagating the Law after his death. In several of his writings, Nichiren Daishonin identifies his own role with that of their leader, Bodhisattva Superior Practices.

consistency from beginning to end The last of the ten factors mentioned in the "Expedient Means" chapter of the Lotus Sutra. It is the integrating factor that unies the other nine in every moment of life.

daimoku (Jpn) Literally, 'title.' 1) The title of a sutra, in particular the title of the Lotus Sutra, Myoho-renge-kyo. 2) The invocation of Nam-myoho-renge-kyo in Nichiren Daishonin's Buddhism.

Daishonin   (Jpn) Literally, 'great sage.' In particular, this honoric title is applied to Nichiren to show reverence for him as the Buddha who appears in the Latter Day of the Law to save all humankind.

devil king of the sixth heaven   The king of devils, who dwells in the highest of the six heavens of the world of desire. He works to obstruct Buddhist practice and delights in sapping the life force of other beings. He is also regarded as the manifestation of the fundamental darkness inherent in life. Also called the heavenly devil.

Eagle Peak   (Skt Gridhrakuta) Also, Vulture Peak. A mountain located to the northeast of Rajagriha, the capital of Magadha in ancient India, where Shakyamuni is said to have expounded the Lotus Sutra. Eagle Peak also symbolizes the Buddha land or the state of Buddhahood. In this sense, the 'pure land of Eagle Peak' is often used.

five elements   The five constituents of all things in the universe, according to ancient Indian belief. They are earth, water, fire, wind and space. The first four correspond respectively to the physical states of solid, liquid, heat and gas. Space is interpreted as integrating the other four elements.

four great voice-hearers   Maudgalyayana, Mahakashyapa, Katyayana and Subhuti. See also voice-hearers.

four heavenly kings   Lords of the four quarters who serve Shakra as his generals and protect the four continents.

four noble truths   A fundamental doctrine of early Buddhism, it teaches that (1) all existence is marked by suffering; (2) suffering is caused by craving; (3) by doing away with craving one can gain release from suffering; (4) there is a method for achieving this goal. The method is known as the eightfold path, which enjoins one to cultivate right views, right thinking, right speech, right action, right way of life, right endeavor, right mindfulness and right meditation.

Gohonzon   (Jpn) *Go* means 'worthy of honor' and *honzon* means 'object of fundamental respect.' The object of devotion in Nichiren Daishonin's Buddhism and the embodiment of the Mystic Law permeating all phenomena. It takes the form of a mandala inscribed on paper or on wood with characters representing the Mystic Law as well as the Ten Worlds, including Buddhahood. Nichiren Daishonin's Buddhism holds that all people possess the Buddha nature and can attain Buddhahood through faith in the Gohonzon.

gongyo   (Jpn) Literally, 'assiduous practice.' In the Daishonin's Buddhism, it means to chant Nam-myoho-renge-kyo and portions of the "Expedient Means" and "Life Span" chapters of the Lotus Sutra. It is performed morning and evening.

Gosho   (Jpn) Literally, 'honored writings.' The individual and collected writings of Nichiren Daishonin.

human revolution   A concept coined by the Soka Gakkai's second president, Josei Toda, to indicate the self-reformation of an individual — the strengthening of life force and the establishment of Buddhahood — that is the goal of Buddhist practice.

Jainism   An Indian religion that stresses nonviolence and not killing any forms of life, it teaches the liberation of the soul by right knowledge, right faith and right conduct.

Jambunada Gold   Gold found in the river running through the forest of the Jambu trees in Jambudvipa.

Jetavana Monastery   A monastery in Shravasti where Shakyamuni is said to have lived and taught during the rainy season for the last twenty-five years of his life. It was built as an offering by Sudatta on land provided by Prince Jetri. Along with the Bamboo Grove Monastery in Rajagriha, it was once one of the two main centers of the Buddha's propagation activities.

kalpa   (Skt) An extremely long period of time. Sutras and treatises differ in their definitions, but *kalpas* fall into two major categories, those of measurable and immeasurable duration. There are three kinds of measurable *kalpas*: small, medium and major. One explanation sets the length of a small *kalpa* at approximately sixteen million years. According to Buddhist cosmology, a world repeatedly undergoes four stages: formation, continuance, decline and disintegration. Each of these four stages lasts for twenty small *kalpas* and is equal to one medium *kalpa*. Finally, one complete cycle forms a major *kalpa*.

kosen-rufu   (Jpn) Literally, to 'widely declare and spread [Buddhism].' Nichiren Daishonin defines Nam-myoho-renge-kyo of the Three Great Secret Laws as the law to be widely declared and spread during the Latter Day. There are two aspects of kosen-rufu: the kosen-rufu of the entity of the Law, or the establishment of the Dai-Gohonzon, which is the basis of the Three Great Secret Laws; and the kosen-rufu of substantiation, the widespread acceptance of faith in the Dai-Gohonzon among the people.

ku   (Jpn) A fundamental Buddhist concept, variously translated as nonsubstantiality, emptiness, void, latency, relativity, etc. The concept that entities have no fixed or independent nature.

Kumarajiva (344–413 C.E.) Translator of the Lotus Sutra into Chinese.

Latter Day of the Law   Also, the Latter Day. The last of the three periods following Shakyamuni Buddha's death when Buddhism falls into confusion and Shakyamuni's teachings lose the power to lead people to enlightenment. A time when the essence of the Lotus Sutra will be propagated to save all humankind.

Lotus Sutra   The highest teaching of Shakyamuni Buddha, it reveals that all people can attain enlightenment and declares that his earlier teachings should be regarded as preparatory.

mahasattva   (Skt) A 'great being.' Another term for bodhisattva.

Mystic Law   The ultimate law of life and the universe. The law of Nam-myoho-renge-kyo.

Nam-myoho-renge-kyo   The ultimate law of the true aspect of life permeating all phenomena in the universe. The invocation established by Nichiren Daishonin on April 28, 1253. Nichiren Daishonin teaches that this phrase encompasses all laws and teachings within itself, and that the benefit of chanting Nam-myoho-renge-kyo includes the benefit of conducting all virtuous practices. *Nam* means 'devotion to'; *myoho* means 'Mystic Law'; *renge* refers to the lotus flower, which simultaneously blooms and seeds, indicating the simultaneity of cause and effect; *kyo* means sutra, the teaching of a Buddha.

nayuta and *asamkhya*   (Skt) Ancient Indian numerical units, whose explanations differ according to the source. One source defines them respectively as 10^{11} and 10^{59}.

Nichiren Daishonin   The thirteenth-century Japanese Buddhist teacher and reformer who taught that all people have the potential for enlightenment. He defined the universal Law as Nam-myoho-renge-kyo and established the Gohonzon as the object of devotion for all people to attain Buddhahood. Daishonin is an honoric title that means 'great sage.'

Mahayana   One of two main branches of Buddhism. It calls itself Mahayana or the 'Great Vehicle' because its teachings enable all beings to attain Buddhahood. It lays particular emphasis upon the bodhisattva.

oneness of body and mind   The principle explaining that the two seemingly distinct phenomena of body, or the physical aspect of life, and mind, or its spiritual aspect, are two integral phases of the same entity.

poison–drum relationship   Another term for reverse relationship, i.e., a bond formed with the Lotus Sutra by opposing or slandering it. The expression "poison drum" comes from the Nirvana Sutra, volume 9, which states, "Once the poison drum is beaten, all the people who hear it will die, regardless of whether or not they have a mind to listen to it." Similarly, when one preaches the Lotus Sutra, both those who embrace it and those who oppose it will equally receive the seed of Buddhahood.

pratyekabuddha   One who perceives the twelve-link chain of causation or who awakens to the truth of impermanence by observing natural phenomena. In Buddhism *pratyekabuddha* generally meant those who lived in a time when there was no Buddha but who awakened to the truth through their own efforts.

presentation and mastery   In the "Record of the Orally Transmitted Teachings," the Daishonin states: "The word *presentation* pertains to Kashyapa, to whom the teachings were
presented. The word *master* [or completion] pertains to
Shakyamuni, who acknowledges Kashyapa's mastery of them.
Thus 'presentation and mastery' signifies that Kashyapa and
Shakyamuni Buddha have attained an identical level of
understanding" (GZ, 729).

Purna   One of Shakyamuni's ten major disciples who was known
as the foremost in preaching the Law. Purna belongs to the
last of the three groups of voice-hearers who understood the
Buddha's teaching by hearing "The Parable of the Phantom
City" chapter about their past relationship with Shakyamuni
major world system dust particle *kalpas*.

Revelation   The second of the three divisions of a sutra (preparation, revelation and transmission), a format often used in
interpreting sutras thought to have been formulated by
T'ien-t'ai. Preparation indicates the introductory section,
revelation the part containing the main teaching, and transmission the concluding part. In the case of the Lotus Sutra,
in addition to the entire sutra having these divisions, each
half may be further analyzed into three sections.

Saddharamapundarika Sutra   The earliest Chinese translation of
the Lotus Sutra, consisting of twenty-seven chapters in ten
volumes. This translation (dated 286 C.E.) corresponds with
the Myoho-renge-kyo (406 C.E.) by Kumarajiva in most
respects, except that it contains several parables that the latter omits.

Shakyamuni   Also, Siddhartha Gautama. Born in India (present-
day southern Nepal) about three thousand years ago, he is the

first recorded Buddha and founder of Buddhism. For fifty years, he expounded various sutras (teachings), culminating in the Lotus Sutra.

six paths   The six lower worlds of Hell, Hunger, Animality, Anger, Humanity and Heaven. See Ten Worlds.

tamalapatra   The leaf of the tamala, which is a kind of sandalwood tree.

ten kinds of offerings   Presenting various offerings of flowers, incense, necklaces, powdered incense, paste incense, incense for burning, silken canopies, streamers and banners, clothing and music, and pressing their palms together in reverence.

Ten Worlds   Ten life-conditions that a single entity of life manifests. Originally the Ten Worlds were viewed as distinct physical places, each with its own particular inhabitants. In light of the Lotus Sutra, they are interpreted as potential conditions of life inherent in each individual. The ten are: (1) Hell, (2) Hunger, (3) Animality, (4) Anger, (5) Humanity or Tranquillity, (6) Rapture, (7) Learning, (8) Realization, (9) Bodhisattva and (10) Buddhahood.

Theravada   'Teaching of the Elders.' One of two main branches of Buddhism, together with Mahayana. It teaches that since Buddhahood is almost impossible to attain, one should aim for the lesser goal of arhat, or worthy. Emphasizes a strict adherence to discipline and a literal interpretation of doctrine.

thirty-two distinctive features and eighty characteristics   The remarkable physical characteristics and extraordinary features possessed by Buddhas and bodhisattvas.

three assemblies in two places   A division of the Lotus Sutra according to the location and sequence of the events described in it. The three assemblies are the first assembly on Eagle Peak, the Ceremony in the Air and the second assembly on Eagle Peak. The two places are on Eagle Peak and in the air.

three cycles of preaching   The cycles of preaching, understanding and prediction of enlightenment that Shakyamuni employed in the Lotus Sutra. The cycle is repeated in accord with the different capacities of each of the three groups of voice-hearer disciples.

three obstacles and four devils   Various obstacles and hindrances to the practice of Buddhism. The three obstacles are: 1) the obstacle of earthly desires; 2) the obstacle of karma, which may also refer to opposition from one's spouse or children; and 3) the obstacle of retribution, also obstacles caused by one's superiors, such as rulers or parents. The four devils are: 1) the hindrance of the five components; 2) the hindrance of earthly desires; 3) the hindrance of death, because untimely death obstructs one's practice of Buddhism or because the premature death of another practitioner causes doubts; and 4) the hindrance of the devil king.

three thousand realms in a single moment of life   Also, *ichinen sanzen*. A philosophical system set forth by T'ien-t'ai in his *Great Concentration and Insight*, clarifying the mutually inclusive relationship of the ultimate truth and the phenomenal world. This means that the life of Buddhahood is universally inherent in all beings, and the distinction between a common person and a Buddha is a phenomenal one.

Thus Come One   One of the ten honorable titles for a Buddha, meaning one who has arrived from the world of truth. That is, the Buddha appears from the world of enlightenment and, as a person who embodies wisdom and compassion, leads other beings to enlightenment.

twelve-linked chain of causation   Also called the doctrine of dependent origination, an important part of the teaching of early Buddhism. It illustrates step by step the causal relationship between ignorance and suffering. It is described in the seventh chapter of the Lotus Sutra.

twenty-four–character Lotus Sutra   Words that Bodhisattva Never Disparaging spoke to all people; in Chinese, they comprise twenty-four characters, hence the name. According to "The Bodhisattva Never Disparaging" chapter of the Lotus Sutra, he said, "I have profound reverence for you, I would never dare treat you with disparagement or arrogance. Why? Because you are all practicing the bodhisattva way and are certain to attain Buddhahood."

voice-hearers   Shakyamuni Buddha's disciples. Those who listen to his preaching and strive to attain enlightenment. In this sense. Voice-hearers are also called voice-hearer disciples. Voice-hearers also denote those who hear the teaching of the four noble truths and aim at attaining the state of arhat. See also four great voice-hearers.

wonderful enlightenment   *Myogaku*, the last of the fifty-two stages of bodhisattva practice, indicating the state of Buddhahood.

yojana   (Skt) A unit of measurement used in ancient India, equal to the distance that the royal army was thought to be able to march in a day. Approximations vary as widely as six miles, ten miles and fifteen miles.

Index

three poisons, 176
three powerful enemies, 116–17
three vehicles, 5, 9, 15, 54, 69,
    143, 156–57; unification of,
    165–69. *See also* one vehicle
three virtues of Buddha, 204
T'ien-t'ai, 16, 41, 66, 68, 79, 101,
    113–14, 157, 164, 173
Toda, Josei, 25, 93, 120, 134,
    139–41, 146, 174, 192–94,
    197, 203, 208–09; and attain-
    ing Buddhahood, 99
Toki Jonin, 85
Tokyo, 183
Tolstoy, Leo, 155, 169
two thousand learners and
    adepts, 164, 167; predictions
    of enlightenment for,
    162–63, 187
two vehicles, 18, 34, 75, 112–13,
    128–29, 164; practitioners of,
    36–38, 43

U
United States, 95, 206
Upali, 198

V
Vasubandhu, 18
Vedas, 50
virtues of the Buddha, 204
voice-hearers, 8, 18, 34, 43, 67,
    110–13, 128, 130–31, 134–36,
    143, 156, 158, 165–68, 172,

176, 178,187; and attaining
    Buddhahood, 103, 130;
    awakening of the, 156–58,
    172–73; Buddha's prediction
    of enlightenment for the,
    157, 163–64, 191–92; wisdom
    of, 79. *See also* four great
    voice-hearer disciples
Vorobyova-Desyatovskaya, Mar-
    garita I., research on the
    Lotus Sutra, 151–52

W
wealthy man and his son para-
    ble, 17, 20, 34, 38–41, 66, 69,
    179; T'ien-t'ai's interpreta-
    tion of the, 41–42. *See also*
    parables
Wilson, Bryan, 206
wisdom, 33, 49, 51–52, 54, 58,
    78–80, 131, 104; of the Bud-
    dha, 77–80, 87, 110, 158, 163,
    172, 202–03; cunning, 80
Wittgenstein, Ludwig, 48
Wolferen, Karel Van, 33
women, prophecy of enlighten-
    ment for, 112
working for others' happiness,
    152–53, 156

Y
Yoshichika, Fujiwara no, 14
young people, 178